Crochet Workshop

learn how to crochet with 20 inspiring projects

Erika Knight

quadrille

photography by Yuki Sugiura

Publishing Director Jane O'Shea
Commissioning Editor Lisa Pendreigh
Pattern Checker and Stitch Chart
Illustrator Sally Harding
Creative Director Helen Lewis
Art Direction and Design Claire Peters
Design Assistant Nicola Davidson
Photographer Yuki Sugiura
Stylist Charis White
Illustrators Joy FitzSimmons
and Paul Griffin
Models Chinh Hoang, Kim Lightbody
and Panda
Production Director Vincent Smith
Production Controller Aysun Hughes,
Nikolaus Ginelli

This edition published in 2018
by Quadrille, an imprint of Hardie
Grant Publishing
52–54 Southwark Street
London SE1 1UN
quadrille.com

Text and project designs
© Erika Knight 2012
Photography
© Yuki Sugiura 2012
Artwork, design and layout
© Quadrille 2012

Cataloguing in Publication Data: a catalogue
record for this book is available from the
British Library.

ISBN: 978 1 78713 172 9

Printed in China

It is the simplicity of crochet that inspires me. With just a few basic stitches worked either in lines or round and round, using only a hook and some yarn you can create seemingly endless textures. With only one stitch ever in work on the hook, it is a deceptively simple craft that anyone can master, as well as being conveniently portable.

I love the craft of crochet for its diversity; from the fabulously fine filet and imitating intricate lace of traditional crochet to the extremely oversized contemporary motifs made from the fattest yarns. Over the years, I have collected it all: old-fashioned afghans, vintage edgings, kitsch kitchen accessories and now the rejuvenated crochet motifs that are currently enjoying a fashion moment on the catwalks, fuelling the revival of this fabulous craft.

The projects in this book, *Crochet Workshop*, are very much my take on crochet. This book is not intended as an exhaustive 'wikipedia' on the minutiae of crochet. Instead it is a simple introduction to the craft, to set you on your way to mastering basic techniques, selecting yarns and considering colour palettes. I have pared down the craft to the essentials as I see them with the aim of providing the means to get you crocheting. I believe in conquering just the few working methods that are easy, effective and give the right look I require for a specific design. *Crochet Workshop* is crochet my style.

For me, crochet is about the process as well as the project. In the Materials and Techniques section at the start of this book, I have set out the technical how-to information for the basic crochet methods and stitches, but knowing how to work a particular technique is no use in isolation and really only makes sense once it is put into practice. This is where the Project Workshops come in. In fact, providing you can master the simple techniques of making a foundation chain, working the basic stitches and grasping the concept of turning chains, then you can easily make the first few items in the Project Workshops section of this book. There are twenty projects in all, including essential accessories and timeless homewares – from the basic starter project of a thrifty dishcloth suitable for the beginner crocheter to the more challenging laceweight scarf and colourful patchwork-inspired motif blanket.

Each project provides the chance to practise and perfect a specific technique or two courtesy of a masterclass. It's your choice whether you work your way through the projects sequentially, refining your skills with each masterclass, or dip in and out of the projects at will – either way you will soon become adept at working the basic stitches, shaping with simple increases and decreases, creating enhanced textures with puff stitches, bobble stitches and popcorn stitches and joining in different colours.

Throughout *Crochet Workshop*, all of the projects reflect my personal preference for an unfussy style; simple shapes generally with no extraneous embellishment in which the texture and shade of each yarn – natural fibres and muted colour tones – are integral to my designs. I am, however, exacting about how I make up the final piece: it is essential to take the time to finish a project. But again this doesn't have to be difficult. I have given instructions for the three best methods of seaming together pieces of crochet.

As well as honing the skills given in the Materials and Techniques section and practised in the Project Workshops, I hope that you will enjoy the variety of textures and patterns that can be created with crochet. In the Stitch Library I have included sixteen of my very favourite stitches and motifs. Again, I hope you will be inspired to experiment with different stitch textures and experiment with colours in order to create your own style.

I love the entire process of creating and constructing a crocheted fabric. This book, *Crochet Workshop*, is my interpretation on the craft. I hope that you will share my love for the pastime and, within these pages, find the inspiration to pick up that hook and simply crochet.

Skill levels

In reality, all the projects in this book are unashamedly simple – that's my style. However, each project has been attributed with a skill level in accordance with the Craft Yarn Council of America's rating system in order to let you know what techniques you are mastering as you learn to crochet.

BEGINNER

1 Beginner Projects For first-time crocheters using basic stitches. Minimal shaping.

EASY

2 Easy Projects Using basic stitches, repetitive stitch patterns, simple colour changes and simple shaping and finishing.

INTERMEDIATE

3 Intermediate Projects Using a variety of techniques, such as basic lace patterns or colour patterns, mid-level shaping and finishing.

EXPERIENCED

4 Experienced Projects With intricate stitch patterns, techniques and dimension, such as non-repeating patterns, multi-colour techniques, fine threads, small hooks, detailed shaping and refined finishing.

materials and techniques

Choosing yarns and colours

Yarn has always been an integral part of my work, whether as a consultant to the fashion industry or working within the craft worlds of hand knitting and crochet. When devising a project, the sourcing of materials is always my starting point where the yarn – or indeed the fibre – sets the course the project is to take.

With yarns that range from the whisper-fine to the phenomenally fat, I love the extremes that the craft of crochet allows. Whatever yarn I select, a yarn must be 'fit for purpose' or 'right for the job' as it determines the colour, stitch pattern and texture of the final fabric and therefore informs the entire character of the project. In an exhaustive and exacting process, I swatch up each yarn to accurately analyse how it performs and looks. This is not only one of the most crucial parts of designing but, for me, it is also one of the most pleasurable. It is often a protracted task as I can spend hours playing with texture through fibres, trying to capture the essence of yarns in a design sketch on paper with my HB pencil.

The time invested in this early design stage is, I believe, always repaid as the quality of yarn is inherent in everything I do. This is particularly paramount when creating very simple pieces: how the yarn handles on the crochet hook, the fluidity or firmness of the resulting fabric, how the fabric will hang or drape, all of this must work together for a project to be truly successful. For many makers, the choice of yarn is either an overlooked part of the process as they speed to the prize of the finished project or is entrusted wholly to the prescriptive pattern instructions.

From string to cashmere, I love the performance of natural fibres. I tend to use natural yarns because of their inherent characteristics – they keep the wearer warm in winter yet cool in summer, wicking moisture away from the skin. Moreover natural fibres are soft, comfortable to wear and not without the hint of luxury that comes only from wearing nature's finest.

For the projects in this book, I have chosen a variety of yarns for their unique textures. Primarily, I have selected animal fibres, including the softest baby alpaca, robust extra-fine merino wool, pure British wool as well as voluminous light-weight wools. Alongside these luxurious animal fibres, sit a small selection of the best natural plant fibres: the versatile staple, mercerised cotton, and the most ancient of the plant fibres, the exquisite linen.

As with selecting fibres, when choosing colours my natural inclination is to steer towards natural shades. The soft tones characteristic of natural yarns enhance the understated simplicity of what I aim to achieve in my designs and provide a solid base to any palette. That said, perversely, I also love to play with 'pops' of stronger colour that add energy to an overall colour scheme. I find this approach works particularly well when designing for the home. In fact, putting together a colour story now feels like second nature to me. The Stripe Cushions on pages 64–67, for example, incorporate 'pops' of teal, fuchsia and chartreuse to enliven on otherwise neutral background of brown, ecru and taupe.

Likewise, throws provide a great opportunity to work with random and eclectic colours to create an individual statement piece. Alternatively, for an elegant timeless heirloom that would suit most sensibilities, throws can be worked in several toning shades or, for the more colour-confident, a striking, dynamic two-colour palette never fails, black and ecru being my favourite. But let's not forget the naturally exquisite single colour, which can instantly become a classic piece. Colour dilemmas we all identify with, no doubt.

Not only am I passionate about designing with yarns, I also believe in promoting the natural, sustainable origins of wool. In creating my Erika Knight Yarn Collection, I am supporting both the British hill farmers and the British textile industry while at the same time creating the ultimate hand-knitting yarns in British wool.

09 brooches

Yarns: fine

The cyclical nature of fashion has seen lace return to the fore. Laceweight and other fine yarns are becoming increasingly popular as gossamer-spun silks and mohairs create contemporary yet classic shawls, scarves and throws. Crochet originally emulated intricate medieval lacework, exquisite textiles in fine cotton and linen threads. Edgings, accessories and homewares were especially popular; one can only covet these pieces, which now mainly reside in textile galleries.

Right Fine and classic crochet linen; its inherent characteristic is its ancient, natural beauty. Linen yarn is an absolute favourite of mine. (Anchor Artiste Linen); **Below** A crochet classic, mercerised cotton, its subtle sheen and compact surface creates firm, precise stitches (Yeoman Yarns Cotton Cannele 4-Ply); **Opposite (from top to bottom)** An alpaca–merino blend yarn (Rowan Fine Lace), delicate and ethereal, tones with two shades of mercerised cotton (Yeoman Yarns Cotton Cannele 4-Ply).

Yarn weight: lace
lace, fingering and 10-count crochet thread
Average crochet tension: 32–42 treble crochet stitches to 10cm
Recommended hook sizes: 1.5–2.25mm

Yarn weight: super fine
sock, fingering and baby
Average crochet tension: 21–32 double crochet stitches to 10cm
Recommended hook sizes: 2.25–3.5mm

Yarn weight: fine
sport and baby
Average crochet tension: 16–20 double crochet stitches to 10cm
Recommended hook sizes: 3.5–4.5mm

(These are the most commonly used tensions and hook sizes for these yarn categories.)

Yarns: medium

Probably the most popular of all yarn weights, medium yarns are easy to work with and readily available. This range consists of double knitting, light worsted, aran, worsted and afghan weight yarns. Over the years, medium yarns have been the entry route to crochet for many crafters. Medium-weight yarns are generally smooth to work with and give good stitch clarity, yet often they can create a less fluid fabric. With crochet especially, it is great to experiment with different weights of yarn using the same stitches to achieve just the right fabric.

 Yarn weight: light
double knitting and light worsted
Average crochet tension: 12–17 double crochet stitches to 10cm
Recommended hook sizes: 4.5–5.5mm

 Yarn weight: medium
aran, worsted and afghan
Average crochet tension: 11–14 double crochet stitches to 10cm
Recommended hook sizes: 5.5–6.5mm

(These are the most commonly used tensions and hook sizes for these yarn categories.)

Above (from left to right) My very own worsted spun aran-weight wool in hanks (Erika Knight Vintage Wool); **Opposite (clockwise from top left)** A glorious jumble of medium-weight yarns, including a pure baby-alpaca yarn (Rowan Baby Alpaca DK), a cotton-and-silk-blend yarn (Rowan Savannah), and a chain yarn consisting of a blend of merino, baby alpaca and nylon (Rowan Lima).

Yarns: fat

I have always created my own yarns by cutting lengths of woven material and plying together several ends of different textures, twisting them to give a more inspiring thread – a great way to recycle surplus natural fabrics or use up stash yarns in an eclectic fashion. Ingrid Wagner has pursued this further and re-energises waste products of the textile industry by using the selvedge edges of looms to great and dramatic effect with huge crochet hooks. The working of crochet on such a large scale creates a whole new vibrancy and way of seeing when working with familiar stitches. I have used Ingrid's gorgeous big yarn, worked on a 25mm hook, to create a simple and homely round rug (see pages 100–3). Similarly, working traditional crochet motifs in my own voluminous Maxi Wool, the simple kimono-shape cardigan has taken on the appearance of extreme, overscaled lace (see pages 136–41).

Opposite (clockwise from top) Finer yarns can be plyed together to create a fat 'supa' yarn by simply working with two or three strands together; make a continuous yarn by cutting fabric into strips (see masterclass, page 98), this is made easier if the fabric is washed beforehand to remove any stiff dressing applied in the manufacturing process; a chunky weight pure wool yarn from my own collection (Erika Knight Maxi Wool); **Above** A unique blend of 100% totally British wool, which has been steam finished to enhance its volume, softness and handle (Erika Knight Maxi Wool).

 Yarn weight: bulky
chunky, craft and rug
Average crochet tension: 8–11 double crochet stitches to 10cm
Recommended hook sizes: 6.5–9mm

 Yarn weight: super bulky
super chunky, bulky and roving
Average crochet tension: 5–9 double crochet stitches to 10cm
Recommended hook sizes: 9mm and larger

(These are the most commonly used tensions and hook sizes for these yarn categories.)

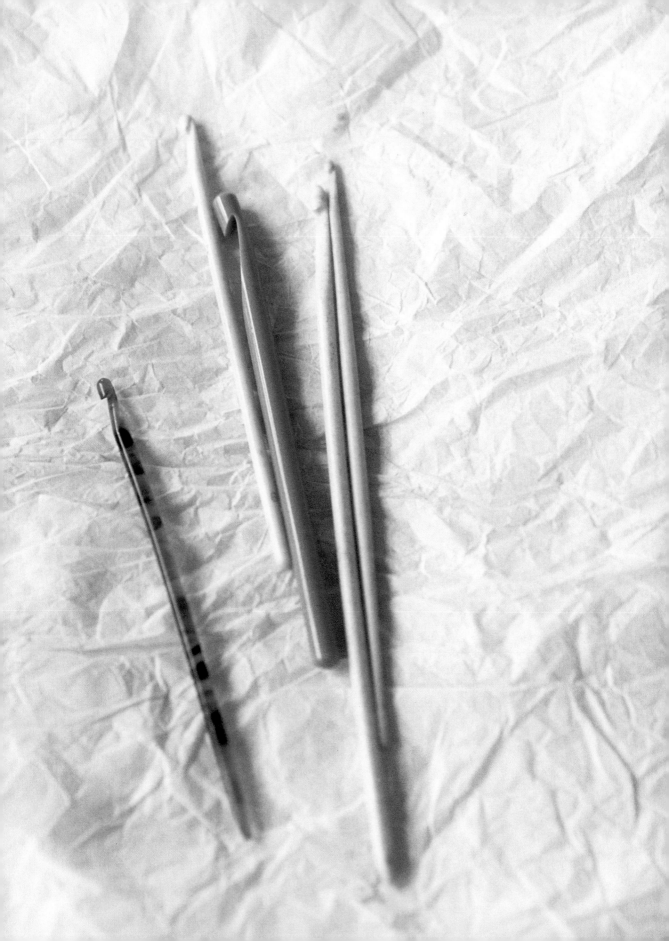

Equipment

Only the minimum of equipment is required to crochet but absolutely essential is the crochet hook, a deceptively simple yet precision engineered piece of equipment. The smallest steel hooks designed for intricate lacework start at 0.75mm and go up to 3.50mm. The most commonly used hooks start at size 3.50mm and go up to 10mm, but even larger hooks are available for 'extreme' crochet. Available in a variety of materials as well as sizes, choose the crochet hook that not only feels most comfortable in your hand but also suits your chosen yarn.

Hooks The constituent parts of a crochet hook are the tip, throat, shank, grip and handle. The rounded tip allows the hook to pass through smoothly when inserted into a stitch or space. Sat just below the tip, the throat of the hook is the crook that catches the working yarn. The shank is the part of the hook that determines the size of the stitches being worked; the size of the hook relates to the diameter of the shank. The grip is where you place your thumb and forefinger, depending on which method you use to hold the hook (see page 21), with the rest of the handle helping to maintain the overall balance of the hook.

Aluminium Hooks are most commonly made from aluminium in a broad range of sizes.

Plastic Coloured plastic hooks are becoming increasingly popular – especially for larger sizes – as they are lighter, more flexible and feel warmer to the touch than aluminium.

Steel The smallest hooks are often made in steel as this metal gives a fine finish and superior strength. A steel hook is the ideal choice of hook for projects worked in fine linen and cotton.

Wood and bamboo Decorative hooks made from hardwoods can sometimes be found, but can feel heavy. Bamboo is more common but due to its inherent characterstics, bamboo hooks are often less smooth than those made from other materials.

Sizing A hook's size correlates to the diameter measurement taken around the shank. In the UK, this is given in millimetres. When checking a hook using a size gauge, the shank fit snugly into the correct size hole. Measurements do vary slightly depending on the manufacturer, so it is always sensible to crochet and measure a tension swatch (see page 41) before beginning a project to ensure you are using the correct size hook.

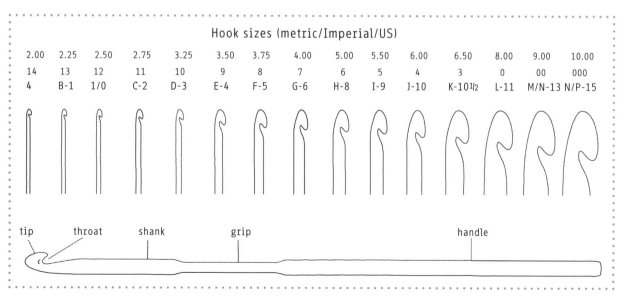

Hook sizes (metric/Imperial/US)

2.00	2.25	2.50	2.75	3.25	3.50	3.75	4.00	5.00	5.50	6.00	6.50	8.00	9.00	10.00
14	13	12	11	10	9	8	7	6	5	4	3	0	00	000
4	B-1	1/0	C-2	D-3	E-4	F-5	G-6	H-8	I-9	J-10	K-10½	L-11	M/N-13	N/P-15

tip   throat   shank   grip   handle

Making a slip knot

To begin to crochet, you need to make a slip knot on the hook. Unlike knitting, there is only ever one stitch on the hook at any one time and the slip knot is the starting point for all stitches that go to make up the finished work.

1 About 15cm from the end of the yarn make a loop by taking the short end over the yarn and then letting the end hang down behind the loop formed.

2 Insert the hook from right to left under the yarn and draw it through the loop, as shown.

3 Pull down on both ends of the yarn. The knot will slide up and tighten around the hook.

1
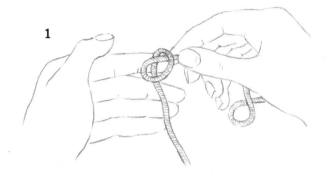

2
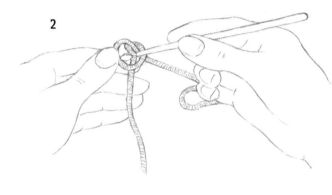

3
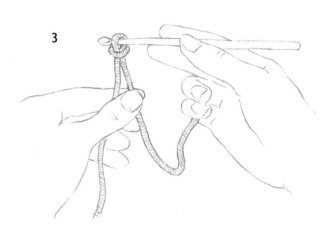

Holding the hook

Crochet is so simple because all you need to do is hold one hook and work one stitch at a time. There are two ways to hold the hook, so try out both of them and see which you find more comfortable.

Pencil grip
Hold the hook as if it were a pencil. Grasp the flat part of the hook between your thumb and forefinger and have the stem resting across the curve between your thumb and forefinger.

Knife grip
Hold the hook as if you were using a knife. Grasp the flat part of the hook between your thumb and forefinger but have the back of your hand on top of the hook with the stem under your palm.

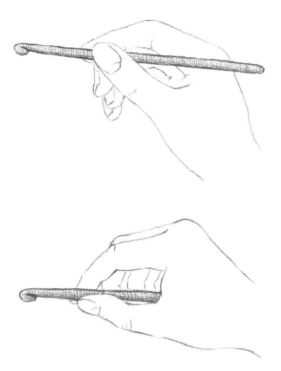

Left-hand method

Crocheting with the left hand is exactly the same as with the right hand but with the hook and yarn position reversed; hook in the left hand, yarn wrapped around the right hand.

Controlling the yarn

The way you hold the yarn allows it to flow from the ball with the right amount of tension applied. There are two methods to try: the forefinger method and the middle finger method. Again, try both of them and see which you find most comfortable.

Forefinger Method

1 Hold the hook with the slip knot in your right hand. Take the working yarn (the end attached to the ball) between the little finger and the next finger and wrap it clockwise around your little finger.

2 Take the yarn under the next two fingers and over and around the forefinger.

3 Hold the yarn, beneath the slip knot, between the thumb and middle finger of your left hand. Now raise your forefinger. You are now ready to crochet, working with the yarn between the hook and your forefinger.

1

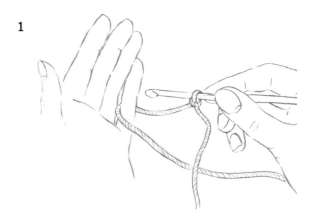

2

3

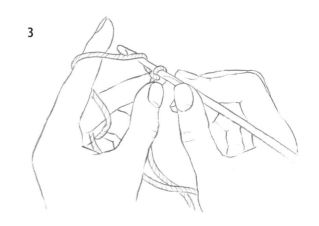

Middle Finger Method

1 Hold the hook with the slip knot in your right hand. Take the working yarn (the end attached to the ball) between the little finger and the next finger and wrap it clockwise around your little finger.

2 Take the yarn across your other fingers and over the top of your forefinger.

3 Hold the yarn, just below the slip knot, between the thumb and forefinger of your left hand. Now raise your middle finger to control the yarn and pull it through your fingers. You will be working with the yarn between the hook and your middle finger.

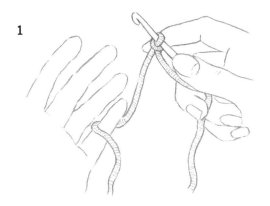

1

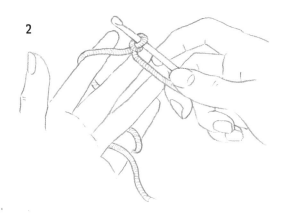

2

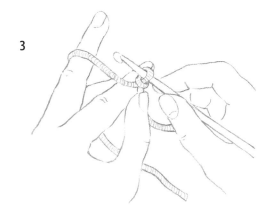

3

Tensioning the tail

It is necessary to apply some tension to the tail end of the yarn, otherwise you'll find yourself attempting to crochet in mid air. Use either the second or the third finger and thumb of your left hand to pull gently on the tail end of the yarn by pinching it just below the hook.

Making a foundation chain

Crochet most often starts with a series of chain stitches, which are used to make the first row: this is called the foundation chain. It needs to be worked loosely and evenly to ensure that the hook can enter each loop on the first row. You may find it tricky to achieve an even tension at first but, again, you may need to practise this several times.

1 Holding the slip knot with the left hand and keeping the yarn taut between the hook and your raised finger, push the hook forwards and twist it towards you as you take it under, behind and then over the yarn so that the yarn wraps around the hook and is caught in the slot. This is called yarn round hook (yrh).

2 Draw the yarn through the loop on the hook, keeping the yarn under an even tension. This forms a new loop on the hook and makes one chain stitch. The new loop should be loose enough to allow the next chain to be drawn through easily.

3 Holding the chain nearest the hook with the thumb and middle finger, repeat steps 1 and 2 until you have the required number of chains. Do not count the loop on the hook. All the chain stitches should be the same size.

1

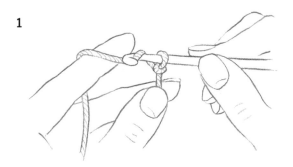

2

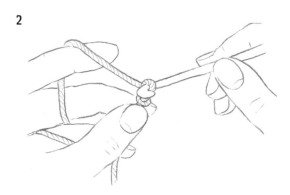

3

Counting chains

When working from any pattern you will need to make a given number of chains to create the foundation row. In order to count the chains accurately, it is important to be able to recognise the formation of each chain.

The front of a chain
The front of the chain looks like a series of V shapes made by the yarn. Each V is a chain loop sitting between the chain loop above and the chain loop below. The first chain made will have the slip knot sitting directly underneath it. The surface of the chain is smooth on this front side. Stitches should be counted from this side of the chain wherever possible.

The reverse of a chain
The reverse of the chain has a row of bumps that have been created by the yarn. These bumps sit behind the V and run in a vertical direction from just above the slip knot to the hook. The surface of the reverse of the chain is more textural than the front side.

Counting chains
When counting chains, do not include the stitch on the hook. This is because, at all times, a loop remains on the hook up to the point where you fasten off. To make counting chains easier when working a large number of chains, it is a good idea to place stitch markers at predetermined intervals, such as after every 10 or 20 stitches.

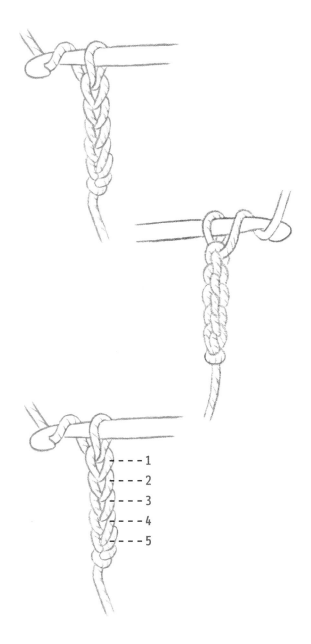

Working loose stitches

When making chains, or indeed any stitches, make sure each stitch is taken up onto the thicker part of the hook (the shank) before moving on to the next one. If you work the stitches on the thinner part of the hook (the throat) they will be tight and it will be difficult to place the hook into them on subsequent rows.

Working slip stitch

There are five basic stitches used within crochet. Slip stitch is the most basic of all those five. It is used mostly for joining rows when you are working in the round and for decreasing. However, it is an excellent stitch to start with and for you to practise the skills of holding the hook and the yarn.

1 Make a foundation chain of evenly worked chain stitches. Identify the second chain from the hook.

2 Insert the hook from front to back under the top loop of the second chain.

1

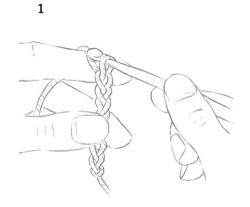

2

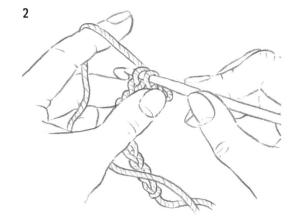

3 Take the hook under, behind and then over the yarn (yarn round hook — yrh) so the yarn is caught by the hook.

4 Draw the yarn back through the two loops now on the hook. You will now have one loop on the hook and this completes the slip stitch.

5 To continue working slip stitch, insert the hook into the next chain and repeat steps 3 and 4.

3

4

5

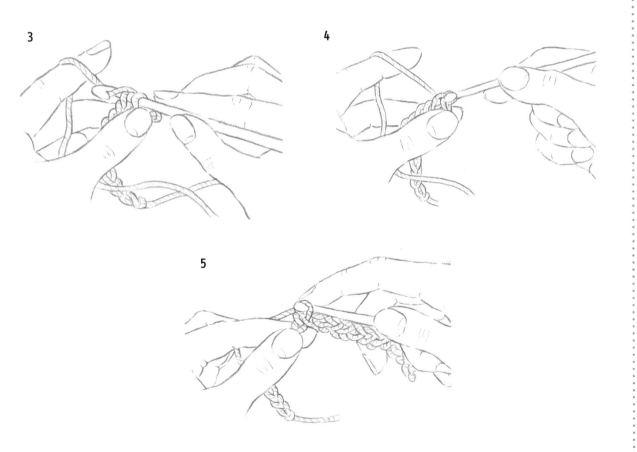

Working double crochet

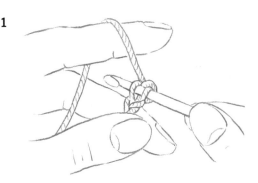

Double crochet is a core stitch to learn. Once mastered, double crochet and the other basic stitches can be used in combination to make a variety of decorative stitches. Double crochet is one of the easiest basic stitches.

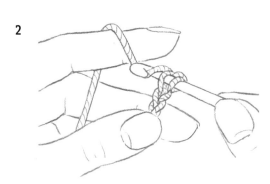

1 Once you have worked the foundation chain, identify the second chain from the hook. Insert the hook from front to back under the top loop of the second chain.

2 Take the yarn round the hook.

3 Draw the yarn back through the first loop on the hook. You will now have two loops on the hook.

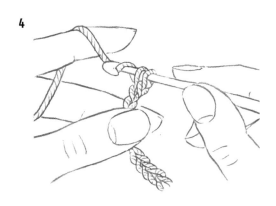

4 Take the yarn round the hook

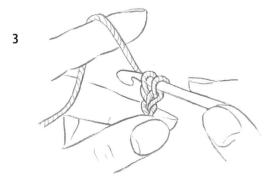

5 Draw the yarn through both loops on the hook. You now have one loop on the hook and this completes the stitch.

6 Work one double crochet into each chain of the foundation chain. At the end of the row, turn the work so the yarn is behind the hook. Work one chain stitch. This is called the turning chain and does not count as a stitch (see page 36).

7 Insert the hook from front to back under both top loops of the first double crochet at the beginning of the row.

8 Work a double crochet into each stitch of the previous row. Make sure you work into the last double crochet stitch of the row below but not the turning chain.

5

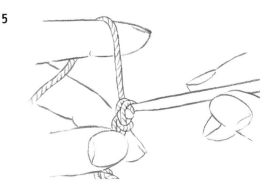

6

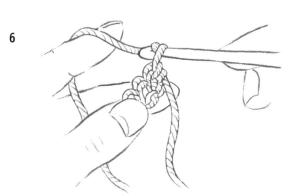

7

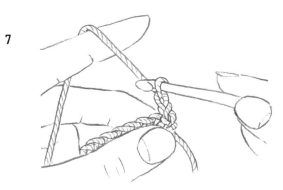

8

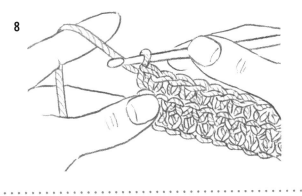

Turning chain

For double crochet
All rows – one chain to turn and then insert hook into first stitch.

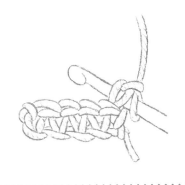

Working half treble crochet

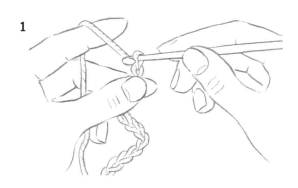

A half treble crochet is between a double and a treble crochet in height. The stitch produces a fabric that is less firm than double crochet but not as open as treble crochet with an attractive ridge across the fabric. The abbreviation for half treble crochet is htr.

1 Make a slip knot about 15cm from the end of the yarn and insert the hook from right to left. Make a foundation chain.

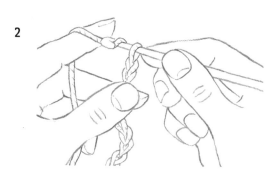

2 Once you have worked the foundation chain, take the yarn round the hook. Identify the third chain from the hook.

3 Insert the hook from front to back under the top loop of the third chain.

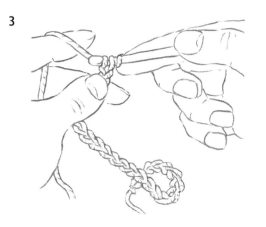

4 Take the yarn round the hook and draw it back through the chain loop. You will now have three loops on the hook. Take the yarn round the hook and draw it through the three loops. This completes the first half treble crochet.

5 Continue in this way, working a half treble into each chain to the end of the row.

6 Turn the work and make a turning chain of two chains. This counts as the first half treble of the next row.

7 Miss the first stitch at the base of the turning chain and work a half treble under both loops of the second stitch in the previous row.

8 Continue in this way, making a half treble into each stitch of the previous row including into the top of the turning chain from the previous row.

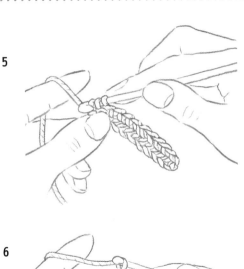

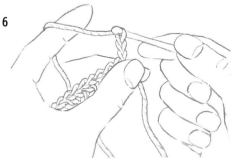

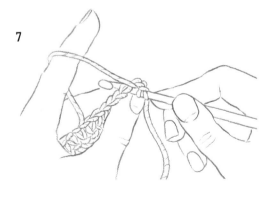

Turning chain

For half treble crochet
Foundation row – miss two chains at beginning of foundation row. Subsequent rows – two chains to turn and then insert hook into second stitch.

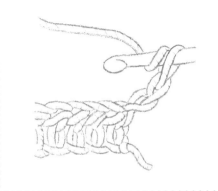

Working treble crochet

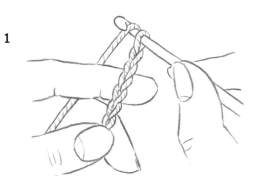

The third of the five basic stitches is treble crochet. Treble crochet stitches are twice as tall as double crochet stitches and work up quickly to form a more open fabric. Treble crochet is the basis of many patterned stitches. The abbreviation for treble crochet is tr.

1 Make a slip knot about 15cm from the end of the yarn and insert the hook from right to left. Make a foundation chain. Once you have worked the foundation chain, take the yarn round the hook. Identify the fourth chain from the hook.

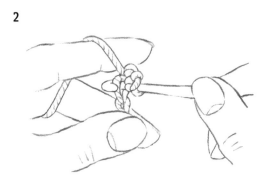

2 Insert the hook from front to back under the top loop of the fourth chain.

3 Take the yarn round the hook and draw it back through the chain loop. You will now have three loops on the hook.

4 Take the yarn round the hook and draw it through the first two loops on the hook. You will now have two loops on the hook.

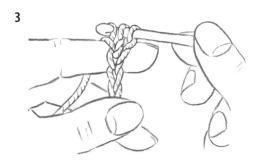

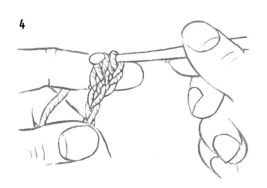

5 Take the yarn round the hook again. Draw the yarn through the remaining two loops on the hook. You will now have one loop on the hook and the stitch is complete.

6 Continue along the foundation chain, working a treble crochet in each chain. This completes one row of treble crochet.

7 To begin the next row, turn the work and make a turning chain of three chain stitches. This turning chain counts as the first stitch of the row. Now locate the second treble crochet stitch in the previous row.

8 Take the yarn round the hook and insert the hook from front to back under BOTH loops of this second stitch. Repeat steps 3–5. Continue along the row, working a treble crochet under both loops of each treble crochet in the row below. When you reach the end of the row, work the last stitch into the top chain of the turning chain on the previous row.

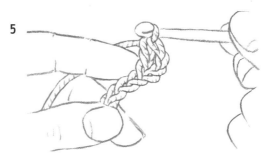

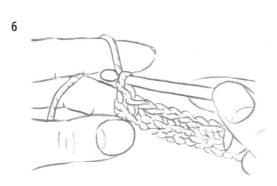

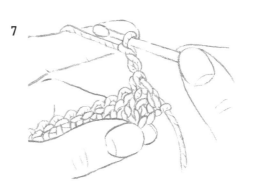

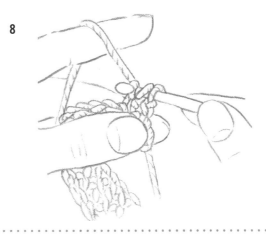

Turning chain

For treble crochet
Foundation row – miss three chains at beginning of foundation row. Subsequent rows – three chains to turn and then insert hook into second stitch.

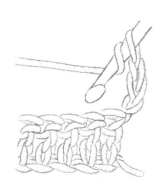

Working double treble crochet

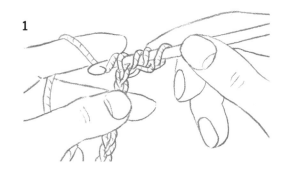

This crochet stitch is three times as tall as a double crochet and forms an open fabric with a looser texture. The abbreviation for double treble crochet is dtr.

1 Make a slip knot about 15cm from the end of the yarn and make a foundation chain. Once you have worked the foundation chain, take the yarn round the hook twice. Identify the fifth chain from the hook. Insert the hook from front to back under the top loop of the fifth chain. Take the yarn round the hook.

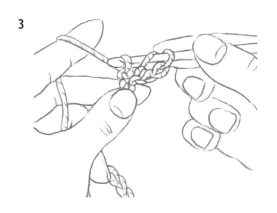

2 Draw the yarn back through the chain loop on the hook. You will now have four loops on the hook.

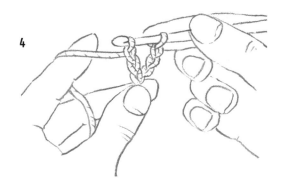

3 Take the yarn round the hook. Draw it through two loops only. There are now three loops on the hook.

4 Take the yarn round the hook. Draw it through two loops only. There are now two loops on the hook.

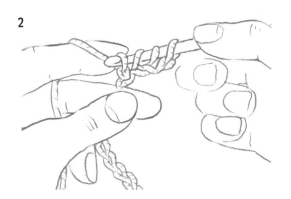

5 Take the yarn round the hook. Draw it through the remaining two loops. You now have one loop on the hook and this completes the stitch.

6 Work one double treble crochet into each chain of the foundation chain.

7 When you reach the end of the row, turn the work so that the yarn is behind the hook. Work four chain stitches. This turning chain counts as the first double treble of the new row. You are now ready to work back in the other direction.

8 Miss the first stitch at the base of the turning chain. Work a double treble into the second stitch inserting the hook under both the top loops of the stitch in the previous row. Continue in this way, working a double treble crochet into each stitch to the end, including the top chain of the turning chain.

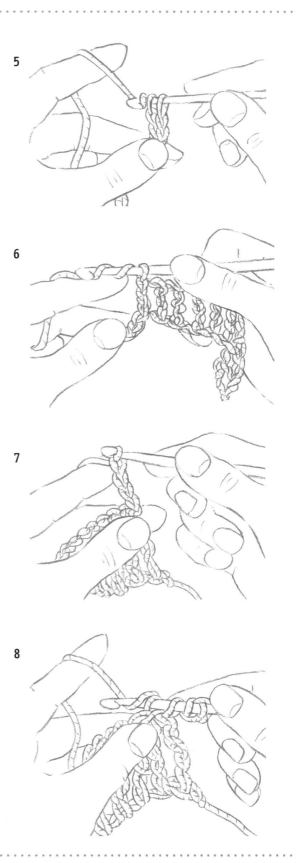

5

6

7

8

Turning chain

For double treble crochet
Foundation row – miss four chains at beginning of foundation row. Subsequent rows – four chains to turn and then insert hook into second stitch.

Working turning chains

When crochet is worked in rows and the work is turned between each row you must add turning chains to bring the hook up to the height of the new row of stitches. Each crochet stitch uses a specified number of chains because the stitches vary in height. You can make a turning chain in two ways and both are explained here.

Turning chain counts as first stitch
1 This is the most common way of making a turning chain. Work to the end of the first row and turn the work. Make the number of chains as instructed in the pattern. Identify the second stitch of the row below, as you are going to work into this, missing the first stitch.

2 Insert the hook from front to back under the top two loops of the second stitch in the row below. By missing the first stitch you have made the turning chain the first stitch of this new row.

3 Work to the end of the row, making a stitch into the top of every stitch on the row below. When you reach the end, make the last stitch into the top of the turning chain from the row below. Working in this way keeps the number of stitches constant and the edges of the work straight.

1

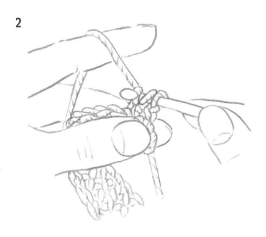

2

3

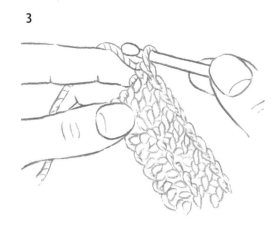

Turning chain does not count as a stitch

1 This method is used for short stitches, such as double crochet. Work to the end of the row and turn the work. Make the number of chains as instructed and identify the first stitch at the beginning of the row.

2 Work the first stitch into the first stitch at the base of the turning chain. Continue to the end of the row and work the last stitch into the last double crochet of the row below, not the turning chain.

1

2

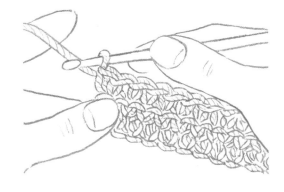

When to turn

You can add the turning chains at the end of the row, before you turn the work, or after you have turned the work and before you begin the new row. Adding at the end makes it easier to count the chains if you need to double-check, while many patterns will instruct you to add at the beginning – the choice is yours.

1

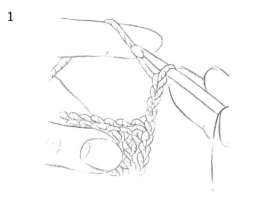

Adding at the end

1 When you reach the end of the row, work the number of chains required and then turn the work. You must turn it from right to left so the yarn is behind the hook in this way you do not twist the chain.

Adding at the beginning

1 When you reach the end of the row, turn the work so the yarn is behind the hook and then add the required number of chains.

2

Working in the round

Instead of working backwards and forwards in horizontal rows, you can work crochet by starting with a central ring and continuing outwards in rounds. When working in rounds, the right side of the work is facing you at all times. The shape of the round is dictated by the decreases and increases that are made as you work the round.

1 Make a short foundation chain of six chains or as instructed in the pattern. Join the chains into a ring by working a slip stitch into the first chain of the foundation chain.

2 Work a starting chain for the first round. The number of chains worked depends on the stitch being used. For treble crochet, for example, you will need to work three chains and this counts as the first treble.

3 Now work the first round of the pattern. Work the stitches into the centre of the ring by inserting the hook into the space in the centre of the ring each time and not into the loops on the foundation chain.

1

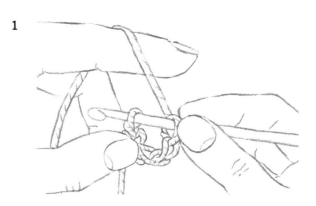

2

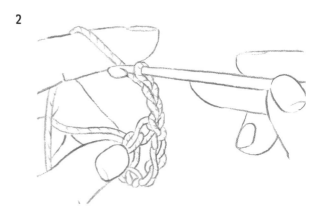

3

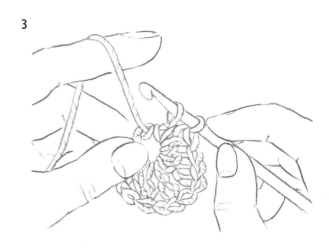

4 To complete the round, you need to join the first and last stitches of the round together. To do this for a round of treble crochet, for example, work a slip stitch into the third chain of the starting chain as shown.

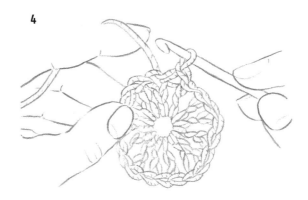

5 Make the starting chain for the next round. For treble crochet, work three chains, which again counts as one treble. To continue, work one treble into the same place. Now work two trebles into each stitch of the previous round. Increasing in this way makes a circular shape. Complete the round by working a slip stitch into the third chain of the starting chain to join the first and last stitches. Working each round as instructed, the number of stitches in each round is increased so that the circle of stitches grows in size.

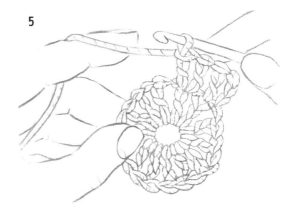

Working into spaces

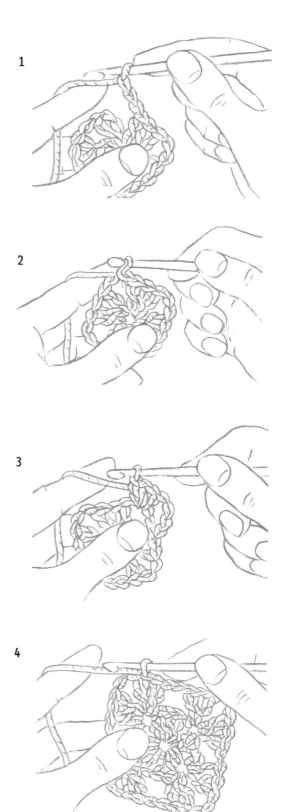

The effects of many crochet designs are formed not just by the stitches but also by where they are placed and the spaces around them. When following a pattern it is often necessary to work into a space made in the previous row or round, rather than working into or around the stitch. Similarly, missing a stitch or two is often integral to a design, particularly if you are working a lacy crochet fabric.

When creating a textured effect by varying the placement of the stitches, the actual stitch being worked is made in exactly the same way as normal – it is only the point where the hook is inserted through the previous rows or rounds that varies. The pattern will state how to place the stitches. Working into the top of a stitch is most common, but working between stitches into the space between them is often called for.

Working into spaces on a square motif
1 Make a foundation chain and slip stitch into the first chain to form a ring. Make 5 chains (this counts as 1 treble and 2 chains). *Work 3 trebles into the ring and then make 2 chains.*

2 Repeat from * to * twice more then make 2 trebles into the ring. Join with a slip stitch into the third of the 5 chains made at the beginning.

3 Slip stitch into the next 2-chain space, make 4 chains, then work 3 half trebles into the same 2-chain space.

4 **Make 1 chain, miss 3 trebles and then work 3 half trebles, 2 chains and 3 half trebles into the next 2-chain space.** Repeat from ** to ** twice more. Make 1 chain, miss 3 trebles and work 2 half trebles into the same space as the four chains at the beginning of the round. Join with a slip stitch into the second chain of the four chains. Continue working rounds in this way following your instructions.

Checking your tension

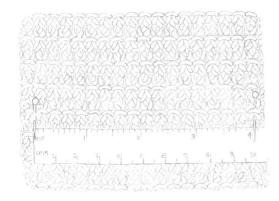

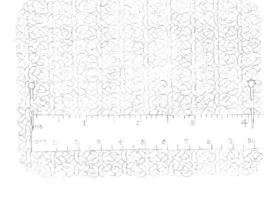

It is crucial to check the tension of your crochet before you embark on any project. Tension is the number of stitches and rows across a particular measurement and is also known as the stitch gauge. The tension determines the measurements of a piece, so if you are making a garment or any other projects that must be a specific size then it is essential you obtain the same number of rows and stitches as stated in the pattern.

If your tension differs from that given in the pattern, your finished piece may be a different size or a distorted shape. A small difference over 10cm can add up to a considerable amount over the complete width of the crocheted item. If your tension is looser or tighter than the one stated in the pattern, a garment will be larger or smaller than the specified size. Taking a moment to check your tension before you start will save a lot of bother and heartache later on.

The size of the stitch depends on the type and weight of the yarn, the size of the hook, the stitch being worked and your control of the yarn. It can also depend on mood. Although for many practising crochet can help to relieve stress, some crocheters experience a tighter tension when anxiety levels are high.

Making a tension swatch
Using the same yarn and hook and stitch that the tension has been measured over in the pattern, crochet a sample at least 13cm square.

Measuring a tension swatch
Smooth out the square on a flat surface. To check stitch tension, place a ruler (a cloth tape measure can be less accurate) horizontally on the fabric and mark 10cm with pins. Count the number of stitches between the pins. To check row tension, place a ruler vertically, mark 10cm with pins and count the number of rows.

Correcting your tension
If the number of stitches and rows is greater than it says in the pattern, your tension is tighter. This can usually be regulated by using a larger hook. If the number of stitches is fewer than the specified number, your tension is looser and you should change to a smaller hook.

A word of caution: your tension may change from that of your sample when crocheting the actual garment, as your crochet tension can alter when working across more stitches. If you are finding it impossible to match the tension stated in the pattern, it is more important to match the stitch tension than the row tension. You can always compensate for the row tension by working more or fewer rows as necessary.

Finishing and seaming

Always take time to finish off your crochet carefully. Here are explanations for what your instrucions mean by 'fastening off' and 'darning in ends', plus a few seaming techniques. There are several ways to join pieces of crochet together, either with a sewing needle or a crochet hook and three of the most popular are given here. For seaming, use the same yarn or a finer yarn matching the project color.

Fastening off
Once you have finished crocheting any piece, you need to fasten off your work securely.

1 When you have finished the final row or round you will be left with one loop on the hook. Cut the yarn approximately 30cm from the hook. Wrap the cut yarn around the hook and draw it through the loop on the hook.

2 Remove the hook and pass the yarn end through the loop. Pull on the end of the yarn to tighten the knot.

Darning in ends
To get rid of any ends that have not been 'enclosed' by working over them, darn the working end of the yarn neatly into the back of the work as shown. Then clip off the yarn end close to the crochet fabric.

1

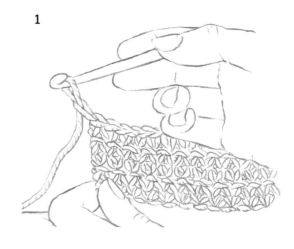

2

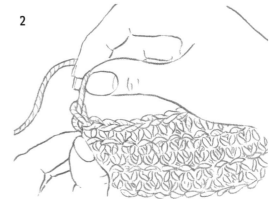

Slip stitch seam

Worked with a hook, the slip stitch seam is a popular method of joining pieces. Place the two pieces to be joined together with the right sides facing. Insert the hook through both pieces at the beginning of the seam, yarn round hook and draw through both pieces and the loop on the hook. Working through both layers slip stitch across the rest of the seam. Take care not to work too tightly as although it is strong and secure, it can be quite rigid and create a slightly bulky seam.

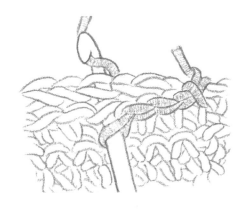

Double crochet seam

A double crochet seam is good for joining straight edges as it makes a less bulky seam. It can also be worked on the right side of the fabric and so can be used to make a feature. It also has the advantage of being slightly stretchy. Place the pieces to be joined together with either right or wrong sides together, as preferred. Insert the hook from front to back through the edges of both pieces, yarn round hook and draw through, complete one double crochet in the usual way and then insert the hook into the next stitch ready to make the next double crochet. Continue in this way to the end of the seam and then fasten off.

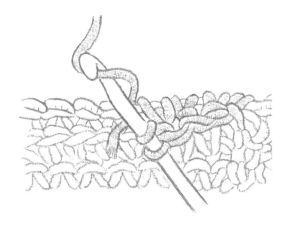

Woven seam

Worked with a blunt-ended needle, I prefer to use a woven seam mostly to give a flatter finish as the straight sides are joined edge to edge. With the right sides of both pieces facing up and the edges to be seamed lined up row to row or stitch to stitch, insert the needle up through the right side of the stitch at the beginning of the seam on piece one. Next insert the needle from the bottom of the stitch to the top of the first stitch at the beginning of the seam of piece two. Then insert the needle up through the next stitch of piece one and then through the second stitch of piece two. Repeat this 'zigzag' process until the seam is completed. Carefully tighten the tension of the stitches as you work so the edges slowly pull together.

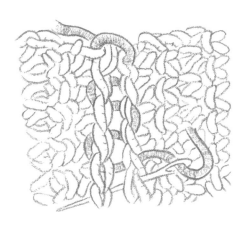

Understanding patterns

When it comes to understanding crochet patterns, there are many shared conventions and terminology. Though designers may use slight variations in style, the same information should always be given. Before purchasing yarn for any project, read through the pattern to ensure you understand exactly what is needed.

Size

For homewares and accessories, patterns usually come in a single size. For garment designs, often a choice of sizes ranging from extra small to extra large are given. Sometimes sizes are given as 'to fit' – the recommended chest or bust measurement for each size – and sometimes they are given as 'actual' – the measurements of the finished piece. Depending on the intended fit of a garment – whether it is loose or tight fitting – these two measurements will not necessarily be the same.

Materials

The pattern specifies what type of yarn is needed for the project, along with the total number of balls. The Asymmetric Cardigan on pages 136–141 is a one-size garment designed to be loose fitting, but when other patterns are for garments that come in different sizes, the number of balls needed for each size will be stated. Also given in the materials list will be the size of crochet hook or hooks required, which could be one or more, as well as any closures, such as buttons and zips, or trims.

Tension

The tension indicates how many stitches and rows you must have to a certain measurement, usually 10cm square. Your tension needs to be correct to achieve the exact dimensions given in a pattern (see page 41 for more on this). Achieving an exact tension is less critical for a throw or a cushion than for a garment, when a different tension will not only affect the finished dimensions but will alter the amount of yarn needed to complete the project.

Pattern instructions

Crochet patterns can be either written or given in a symbol diagram. Sometimes the diagram replaces the written words completely or it is given as well as the line-by-line instructions. The pattern works through the individual elements of the project, giving all the necessary instructions for each part. Every pattern begins with the hook size, shade – or shades – of yarn used, and the number of chains worked for the foundation row or ring. The pattern continues to outline, row-by-row or round-by-round, the stitch pattern to follow and indicates when any shaping or other details, such as buttonholes, should be worked. Follow the instructions for each row or round carefully, paying particular attention to the turning chains.

Abbreviations

The names for stitches and instructions are abbreviated otherwise the patterns would be too long and too difficult to follow. The list of abbreviations is given at the beginning of the pattern and you should check these to make sure you understand each one. It can take a while to become familiar with the language of crochet patterns, so I have listed opposite the most commonly used abbreviations and symbols.

Brackets

When following a pattern, you need to be aware of the different usage of round brackets ( ) and square brackets [ ]. Round brackets are used to contain additional instruction or clarification, such as 3 ch (counts as first tr). Square brackets are used when an instruction has to be repeated a certain number of times; for example, [1 tr in each of next 2 sts, 4 ch] 3 times.

Asterisks

These are used to make patterns shorter and are placed at the beginning of a set of instructions to be repeated. A single asterisk marks the beginning of a pattern repeat sequence. For example, *2 ch, miss 2 ch, 1 tr in next ch; rep from * to end. A double asterisk often indicates a repeat within a series of instructions.

Abbreviations

Following is a list of the most commonly used abbreviations within crochet patterns. In addition, special abbreviations may also be included at the start of a pattern, such as the directions for a specific stitch, which are not necessarily on this list.

alt	alternate
approx	approximately
beg	begin/beginning
CC	contrasting colour
ch	chain(s)
cl	cluster(s)
cm	centimetre(s)
cont	continue/continuing
dc	double crochet(s)
dec	decrease(s)/decreasing
dtr	double treble(s)
foll(s)	follow(s)/following
g	gram(s)
gr	group(s)
htr	half treble(s)
inc	increase(s)/increasing
lp(s)	loop(s)
m	metre(s)
MC	main colour
mm	millimetre(s)
patt(s)	pattern(s)
rem	remain(s)/remaining
rep	repeat(s)/repeating
rnd(s)	round(s)
RS	right side
sp(s)	space(s)
ss	slip stitch
st(s)	stitch(es)
tch	turning chain
tog	together
tr	treble(s)
trtr	triple treble(s)
WS	wrong side
yd	yard(s)
yrh	yarn round hook
[ ]	work instructions within square brackets as many times as directed
( )	contains additional instruction or further clarification

Symbols

Increasingly, crochet patterns are being conveyed in the form of diagrams made up of a series of symbols. Although it can take a while to become familiar with this method, once mastered a diagram gives an immediate visual impression of what the crochet will look like.

Basic stitches

- • slip stitch
- o chain stitch
- + double crochet

 half treble crochet

 treble crochet

 double treble

 triple treble

Shells
Sometimes symbols are grouped into 'V' shapes; this indicates a number of stitches that must be worked into the same stitch or space.

 3-tr shell (worked into same space)

 5-tr shell (worked into a single stitch)

Bobble, cluster, popcorn and puff stitches
The symbols for these stitches often look similar to the stitch itself.

bobbles

clusters

popcorn

puff stitches

Other special symbols

 treble around post from front

treble around post from back

tr2tog

stitch
library

basic
stitches

Make any number of ch for
foundation chain.

Row 1 1 dc in 2nd ch
from hook, 1 dc in each of
remaining ch to end, turn.
Row 2 1 ch (does NOT
count as a stitch), 1 dc in
each dc to end, turn.
Rep 2nd row to form
dc fabric.

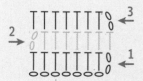

Double Crochet

– the most basic stitch, and
  probably my favourite
– creates a firm, flat fabric
– versatile and reversible
– beautiful for homewares

Make any number of ch for
foundation chain.

Row 1 1 htr in 3rd ch from
hook, 1 htr in each of
remaining ch to end, turn.
Row 2 2 ch (counts as first
htr), miss first htr in row
below, *1 htr in next htr;
rep from * to end, work
last htr in top of 2-ch at
end, turn.
Rep 2nd row to form htr
fabric.

Half Treble Crochet

– a basic and satisfying
  stitch to crochet
– good for when a more
  fluid fabric is needed
– less compact than double
  crochet

Treble Crochet

- the fabric grows really quickly with this stitch
- great when used in combination with other stitches

Make any number of ch for foundation chain.

Row 1 1 tr in 4th ch from hook, 1 tr in each of remaining ch to end, turn.
Row 2 3 ch (counts as first tr), miss first tr in row below, *1 tr in next tr; rep from * to end, work last tr in top of 3-ch at end, turn.
Rep 2nd row to form tr fabric.

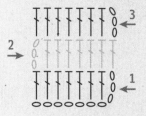

Double Treble Crochet

- a very long variation on the basic crochet stitch
- a highly decorative stitch

Make any number of ch for foundation chain.

Row 1 1 dtr in 5th ch from hook, 1 dtr in each of remaining ch to end, turn.
Row 2 4 ch (counts as first dtr), miss first dtr in row below, *1 dtr in next dtr; rep from * to end, work last dtr in top of 4-ch at end, turn.
Rep 2nd row to form dtr fabric.

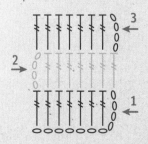

texture stitches

Make an even number of ch for foundation chain.

Row 1 1 dc in 2nd ch from hook, *1 ch, miss 1 ch, 1 dc in next ch; rep from * to end, turn.
Row 2 1 ch (does NOT count as a stitch), 1 dc in first dc, 1 dc in next 1-ch sp, *1 ch, 1 dc in next 1-ch sp; rep from * to last dc, 1 dc in last dc, turn.
Row 3 1 ch (does NOT count as a stitch), 1 dc in first dc, *1 ch, 1 dc in next 1-ch sp; rep from * to last 2 dc, 1 ch, miss 1 dc, 1 dc in last dc, turn.
Rep rows 2 and 3 to form pattern.

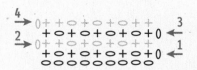

Make an even number of ch for foundation chain.

Row 1 2 dc in 4th ch from hook, *miss 1 ch, 2 dc in next ch; rep from * to end, turn.
Row 2 2 ch, miss first dc, 2 dc in next dc, *miss next dc, 2 dc in next dc; rep from * to end, turn.
Rep row 2 to form pattern.

Woven Stitch

– *one of my favourite stitches*
– *a lovely discrete texture*
– *beautifully rustic when worked in a tweed yarn*

Alternate Stitch

– *an easy and pretty stitch*
– *creates a firm, neat fabric*
– *made by working two double crochets in every other stitch*

Rope Stitch

– a classic stitch in my books
– well suited to baby blankets
– the cellular construction of
  this stitch provides warmth
  and comfort

Make a multiple of 3 ch for foundation chain.

Row 1 1 tr in 4th ch from hook, 1 ch, 1 tr in
next ch, *miss 1 ch, 1 tr in next ch, 1 ch,
1 tr in next ch; rep from * to last ch, 1 tr in
last ch at end, turn.
Row 2 3 ch (counts as first tr), work [1 tr,
1 ch, 1 tr] all in each 1-ch sp to end of row,
1 tr in top of 3-ch at end, turn.
Rep row 2 to form pattern.

Note: This stitch is used for the Texture
Throw on pages 72–5.

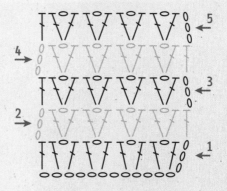

Make a multiple of 8 ch, plus 4 extra, for foundation chain.

Base row (WS) 1 tr in 4th ch from hook, 1 tr in each of remaining ch to end, turn.
Row 1 (RS) 2 ch (counts as first tr), miss first tr, *[1 tr around post of next tr from front] 4 times, [1 tr around each post of next tr from back] 4 times; rep from * to end, 1 tr in top of turning ch at end, turn.
Rows 2, 3 and 4 [Rep 2] 3 times.
Row 5 2 ch (counts as first tr), miss first tr, *[1 tr around post of next tr from back] 4 times, [1 tr around post of next tr from front] 4 times; rep from * to end, 1 tr in top of turning ch at end, turn.
Rows 6, 7 and 8 [Rep 5] 3 times.
Rep rows 1–8 to form pattern.

Note: To work 'around the post' of a treble crochet, wrap the yarn around the hook then insert the hook (either from the front or back) through the work between the stitches in the row below and back out again (either to the front or back) around the stitch to complete the treble.

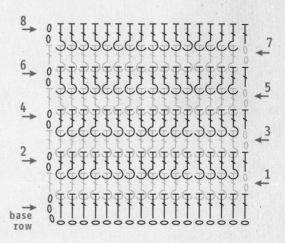

Basketweave Stitch

- *perenially popular stitch*
- *work in really fat yarn to create extreme crochet textures*

clustered and shell stitches

Make a multiple of 2 ch for foundation chain.

1 bobble = [yrh and insert hook in st, yrh and draw a loop through, yrh and draw through first 2 loops on hook] 3 times all in same st, yrh and draw a loop through all 4 loops on hook.

Row 1 1 bobble in 4th ch from hook, 1 ch, *miss 1 ch, 1 bobble in next ch; rep from * to end, turn.
Row 2 3 ch, *1 bobble in next 1-ch sp, 1 ch; rep from * to end, 1 bobble in top of turning chain, turn.
Rep row 2 to form pattern.

Soft Bobble

- bobbles make attractive round yet flat stitches
- identical on both sides so fully reversible
- perfect for homewares or accessories

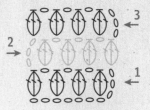

Make a multiple of 3 ch for foundation ch.

Row 1 2 tr in 3rd ch from hook, *miss 2 ch, work [1 dc, 2 tr] all in next ch; rep from * to last 3 ch, miss 2 ch, 1 dc in last ch, turn.
Row 2 2 ch, 2 tr in first dc, *work [1 dc, 2 tr] all in next dc; rep from * to end, 1 dc in turning ch, turn.
Rep row 2 to form pattern.

Ripple Shell Stitch

- a pretty asymmetrical stitch
- rustic yet summery
- particularly lovely when worked in linen

Lace Puff

- *my favourite stitch of all*
- *a soft yarn beautifully enhances this stitch*
- *looks a complex stitch yet is simple to work*

Make a multiple of 6 ch, plus 5 extra, for the foundation chain.

1 puff stitch = [yrh, insert hook in stitch and draw a long loop through] 4 times in same stitch, yrh and draw a loop through all 9 loops on hook.

Row 1 Work [1 tr, 2 ch, 1 tr] all in 4th ch from hook, *miss 2 ch, 1 puff stitch in next ch, 1 ch (this chain closes the puff stitch), miss 2 ch, work [1 tr, 2 ch, 1 tr] all in next ch; rep from * to last ch, 1 tr in last ch, turn.
Row 2 3 ch, 1 puff stitch in first 2-ch sp (between 2 tr), 1 ch, *work [1 tr, 2 ch, 1 tr] all in top of puff stitch (under loop that closes the puff stitch), 1 puff stitch in next 2-ch sp, 1 ch; rep from * to end, 1 tr in 3-ch sp at end of row, turn.
Row 3 3 ch, work [1 tr, 2 ch, 1 tr] all in top of first puff stitch, *1 puff stitch in next 2-ch sp, 1 ch, work [1 tr, 2 ch, 1 tr] all in top of next puff stitch; rep from * to end, 1 tr in 3-ch sp at end of row, turn.
Rep rows 2 and 3 to form pattern.

Note: This stitch is used for the Classic Snood on pages 84–7.

Make a multiple of 10 ch, plus 7 extra, for the foundation chain.

1 cluster = [yrh, insert hook in next stitch, yrh and draw a loop through, yrh and draw through first 2 loops on hook] over the number of sts indicated, yrh and draw a loop through all loops on hook to complete cluster.

Row 1 1 dc in 2nd ch from hook, 1 dc in next ch, *miss 3 ch, 7 tr in next ch (these 7 tr in same chain form a 7-tr shell), miss 3 ch, 1 dc in each of next 3 ch; rep from * to last 4 ch, miss 3 ch, 4 tr in last ch, turn.
Row 2 1 ch, 1 dc in each of first 2 tr, *3 ch, 1 cluster over next 7 sts (that is over next 2 tr, 3 dc, 2 tr), 3 ch, 1 dc in each of next 3 tr (these 3 tr are the 3 centre sts of the 7-tr shell); rep from * to last 4 sts (remaining 2 tr and 2 dc), finishing with 3 ch, 1 cluster over these last 4 sts, turn.
Row 3 3 ch (counts as first tr), 3 tr in top of first 4-tr cluster (under loop that closed the cluster),

*miss 3-ch sp, 1 dc in each of next 3 dc, miss 3-ch sp, 7 tr in top of next cluster (under loop that closed the cluster); rep from * to last 3-ch sp, finishing with miss 3-ch sp, 1 dc in each of last 2 dc, turn.
Row 4 3 ch (counts as first tr), miss first dc, 1 cluster over next 3 sts (that is over next 1 dc, 2 tr), *3 ch, 1 dc in each of next 3 tr (these 3 tr are the 3 centre sts of the 7-tr shell), 3 ch, 1 cluster over next 7 sts (that is over 2 tr, 3 dc, 2 tr); rep from * to last tr, finishing with 3 ch, 1 dc in last tr, 1 dc in top of 3-ch at end of row, turn.
Row 5 1 ch, 1 dc in each of first 2 dc, *miss 3-ch sp, 7 tr in top of next cluster, miss 3-ch sp, 1 dc in each of next 3 dc; rep from * to last 3-ch sp, finishing with miss 3-ch sp, 4 tr in top of 3-ch at end of row, turn.
Rep rows 2–5 to form pattern.

Note: This reversible stitch is used for the Two-Colour Bolster on pages 108–11. See page 111 for the stitch diagram.

Catherine Wheel Stitch

- *this stitch creates an exquisite decorative textile*
- *especially interesting when worked in two or even three colours*

basic motifs

Treble Crochet Square

– *a simple, easy-to-master solid-coloured motif*
– *smooth, pared-down texture, good for understated throws*

Base ring Work 4 ch and join with a slip stitch to first chain to form a ring.
Round 1 (RS) 5 ch (counts as 1 tr and 2-ch sp), [3 tr in ring, 2 ch] 3 times, 2 tr in ring, join with a slip stitch to 3rd of 5-ch at beginning of round. *3 tr along each side of square.*
Note: Do not turn at end of rounds but continue with RS of motif always facing.
Round 2 1 slip stitch in first sp, 7 ch (counts as 1 tr and 4-ch sp), 2 tr in same sp, *1 tr in each tr to next sp, work [2 tr, 4 ch, 2 tr] all in next sp; rep from * twice more, 1 tr in each tr to next sp, 1 tr in same sp as 7-ch, join with a slip stitch to 3rd of 7-ch at beginning of round. *7 tr along each side of square.*
Round 3 Rep round 2. *11 tr along each side of square.*
Round 4 Rep round 2. *15 tr along each side of square.*
Fasten off.

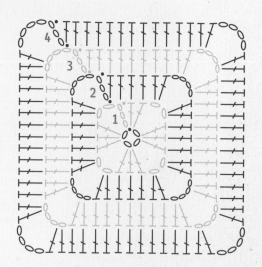

This motif is worked in 3 colours – A, B and C.

Base ring Using A, make 6 ch and join with a slip stitch to first chain to form a ring.
Round 1 (RS) Using A, 3 ch (counts as first tr), 2 tr in ring, [3 ch, 3 tr in ring] 3 times, 3 ch, join with a slip stitch to top of 3-ch at beginning of round. Fasten off.
Note: Do not turn at end of rounds but continue with RS of motif always facing.
Round 2 Using B, join yarn with a slip stitch to any 3-ch sp, 3 ch (counts as first tr), [2 tr, 3 ch, 3 tr] in same 3-ch sp, *1 ch, [3 tr, 3 ch, 3 tr] in next 3-ch sp; rep from * twice more, 1 ch, join with a slip stitch to top of 3-ch at beginning of round. Fasten off.
Round 3 Using C, join yarn with a slip stitch to any 3-ch sp, 3 ch, [2 tr, 3 ch, 3 tr] in same 3-ch sp, *1 ch, 3 tr in next 1-ch sp, 1 ch, [3 tr, 3 ch, 3 tr] in next 3-ch sp; rep from * twice more, 1 ch, 3 tr in next 1-ch sp, 1 ch, join with a slip stitch to top of 3-ch at beginning of round. Fasten off.
Round 4 Using A, join yarn with a slip stitch to any 3-ch sp, 3 ch, [2 tr, 3 ch, 3 tr] in same 3-ch sp, *[1 ch, 3 tr in next 1-ch sp] twice,
1 ch, [3 tr, 3 ch, 3 tr] in next 3-ch sp; rep from * twice more, [1 ch, 3 tr in next 1-ch sp] twice, 1 ch, join with a slip stitch to top of 3-ch at beginning. Fasten off.

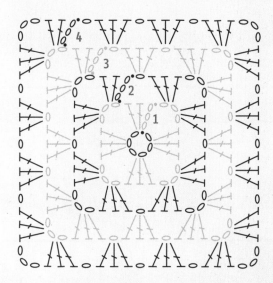

Note: This motif is used for the centre of the Traditional Motif Throw on pages 112–15, which is worked in cotton. Traditionally the motif is worked in wool and sometimes with 2-chain rather than 3-chain corners.

Traditional Square

- *timeless classic crochet motif*
- *endless colourway possibilities*
- *equally effective when made in wool or cotton*

Hexagon

– lovely motif for a patchwork- type throw or bedcover – pin out the finished motifs at the six corners and gently steam to sharpen the shapes

This motif is worked in 2 colours – A and B.

Base ring Using A, make 4 ch and join with a slip stitch to first chain to form a ring.
Round 1 (RS) 3 ch (counts as first tr), 1 tr in ring, [1 ch, 2 tr in ring] 5 times, 1 ch, join with a slip stitch to top of 3-ch at beginning of round.
Note: Do not turn at end of rounds but continue with RS of motif always facing.
Round 2 1 slip stitch in first tr, 1 slip stitch in next ch, 3 ch (counts as first tr), *1 tr in each of next 2 tr, work [1 tr, 1 ch, 1 tr] in next 1-ch sp; rep from * 4 times more, 1 tr in each of next 2 tr, 1 tr in last 1-ch sp, 1 ch, join with a slip stitch to top of 3-ch at beginning of round.
Round 3 Using B, 3 ch (counts as first tr), 1 tr in each tr to first 1-ch sp, work [1 tr, 1 ch, 1 tr] in first 1-ch sp, *1 tr in each tr to next 1-ch sp, work [1 tr, 1 ch, 1 tr] in next 1-ch sp; rep from * to end, join with a slip stitch to top of 3-ch at beginning of round.
Rounds 4 and 5 [Rep round 3] twice.
Fasten off.

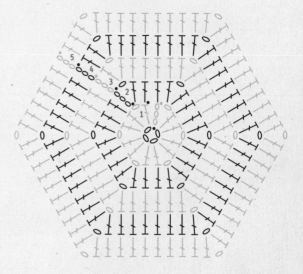

Star Circle

*– worked with ease
in only four rounds
– attractive centre star
shape to show off three
contrasting colours
– perfect simple shape
for coasters*

This motif is worked in 3 colours – A, B and C.

Base ring Using A, make 6 ch and join with a
slip stitch to first chain to form a ring.
Round 1 (RS) 4 ch (counts as first dtr), 2 dtr
in ring, [1 ch, 3 dtr in ring] 5 times, 1 ch, join
with a slip stitch to top of 4-ch at beginning
of round, turn.
Round 2 (WS) 1 ch, [1 dc in next 1-ch sp, 6
ch] 6 times, join with a slip stitch to first dc.
Fasten off.
Round 3 (WS) With WS facing, join B with a
slip stitch to a 7-ch sp, 2 ch, work [1 htr, 2 tr,
3 dtr, 2 tr, 1 htr] in each 7-ch sp to end, join
with a slip stitch to first htr, turn. *6 petals.*
Fasten off.
Round 4 (RS) With RS facing, join C to first
htr of a petal, 4 ch (counts as first dtr), *1
tr in each of next 2 tr, 1 htr in each of next
3 dtr, 1 tr in each of next 2 tr, 1 dtr in each
of next 2 htr; rep from * to end, but omitting
last dtr at end of last repeat, join with a slip
stitch to top of 4-ch at beginning of round.
Fasten off.

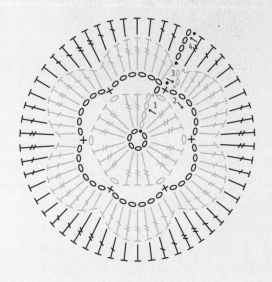

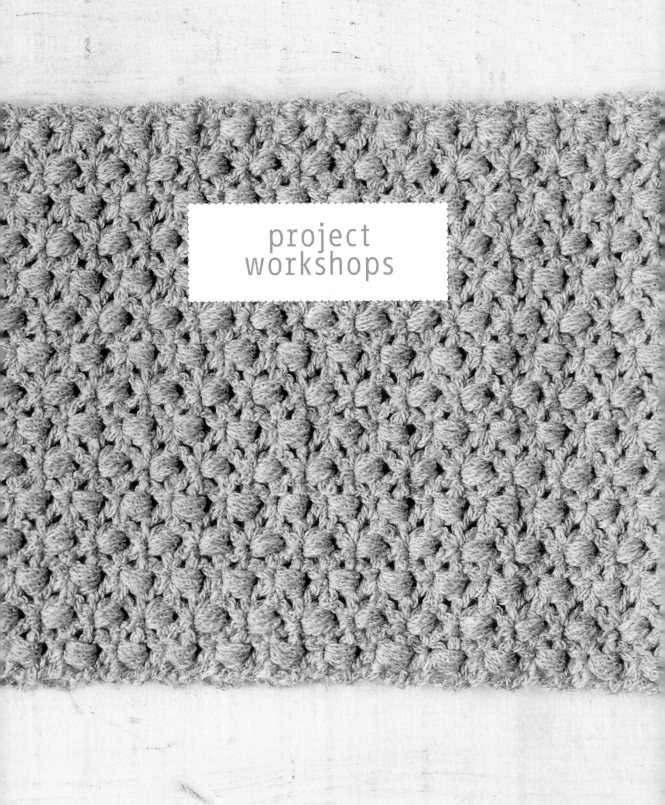

project
workshops

Simple dishcloth

A small yet practical project to get you started with crochet. Making this cloth is the ideal way to practise the basic crochet stitch, double crochet. While the main cloth is worked in double crochet, the contrasting stripes are added to the cloth's surface in slip stitch, a very easy form of crochet embroidery.

Skill level...

BEGINNER

In this project you will learn...
Practising double crochet
Working slip stitch surface embroidery

Stitches used...
Double crochet; Surface slip stitch

Size
Approximately 25cm wide x 30cm long

Materials
Rowan Handknit Cotton, a double-knitting-weight
   cotton yarn, in 2 colours:
     A 2 x 50g balls in taupe (253 Tope)
     B 1 x 50g ball in green (344 Pesto)
5mm crochet hook

Tension
14 dc and 19 rows to 10cm measured over double crochet using a 5mm hook.

Abbreviations
See page 45.

To make dishcloth
Foundation chain Using a 5mm hook and A, make 36 chain.
Row 1 1 dc in 2nd ch from hook, 1 dc in each of remaining ch to end, turn. *35 sts.*

Row 2 1 ch (does NOT count as a stitch), 1 dc in each dc to end, turn. *35 sts.*
Repeat row 2 until work measures 30cm (approximately 56 rows).
Fasten off.

To finish
Weave in any loose ends.
Lay work out flat and gently steam on wrong side.

Masterclass

Adding surface stripes
First stripe Work the first stripe in surface slip stitches between the 2nd and 3rd rows from the bottom edge of the dishcloth as follows: Using a 5mm hook and B, make a slip knot. Remove the hook from slip knot, then insert hook through the dishcloth from the right side of your work one stitch in from the edge, pick up the slip knot again and pull it through to the right side. Keeping the yarn at the wrong side of your work, continue as follows – *insert hook through dishcloth between next 2 stitches, yarn round hook at back of work and pull yarn through dishcloth and loop on hook in one movement. Repeat from * across width of dishcloth, finishing one stitch in from the edge. Fasten off.
Second stripe Work as for the first stripe, but between the 3rd and 4th rows from the top edge of the dishcloth.
Third stripe Work as for the first stripe, but between the 5th and 6th rows from the top edge of the dishcloth.

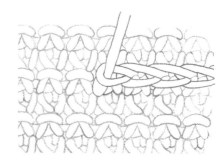

Stripe cushions

A simple square cushion cover made in double and treble crochet and worked in varying widths of stripes and colours. The back is soft corduroy fabric but could be worked in crochet, too.

Skill level

BEGINNER

In this project you will learn
Practising double and treble crochet
Working double crochet into the tops of treble crochet stitches
Working treble crochet stitches into the tops of double crochet stitches
Joining in new colours for stripes, see masterclass on page 67

Stitches used
Double crochet; Treble crochet

Size
Size of finished cushion
Approximately 40cm square
Actual size of crocheted cushion front
Approximately 40cm x 40cm

Materials
Stripe 1 cushion (mostly neutral stripe)
Rowan Cotton Glacé or Rico Essentials Cotton DK, a double-knitting-weight cotton yarn, or any other standard DK yarn in 6 colours:
- A 1 x 50g ball in dark brown
- B 1 x 50g ball in ecru
- C 1 x 50g ball in taupe
- D 1 x 50g ball in light beige
- E 1 x 50g ball in lime green
- F 1 x 50g ball in bright pink

Stripe 2 cushion (all colour stripe)
Rowan Cotton Glacé or Rico Essentials Cotton DK, a double-knitting-weight cotton yarn, or any other standard DK yarn in 9 colours:
- A 1 x 50g ball in dark brown
- B 1 x 50g ball in ecru
- C 1 x 50g ball in taupe
- D 1 x 50g ball in light beige
- E 1 x 50g ball in lime green
- F 1 x 50g ball in bright pink
- G 1 x 50g ball in purple
- H 1 x 50g ball in green
- J 1 x 50g ball in turquoise

Both cushions
3.5mm crochet hook
43cm square of fabric for backing, such as light-weight corduroy or linen, and matching thread
Feather cushion pad to fit finished cushion cover

Tension
17 stitches and 10 rows to 10cm measured over treble crochet using a 3.5mm hook.

Abbreviations
See page 45.

Special pattern note
Pay careful attention to how to work double crochet into a row of treble crochet stitches (as in row 5 of the Stripe 1 Cushion or row 3 of the Stripe 2 Cushion) and also how to work treble crochet into a row of double crochet stitches (as in row 7 of the Stripe 1 Cushion or row 4 of the Stripe 2 Cushion).

Rows 15, 16 and 17 Using A, work in tr.
Rows 18 and 19 Using D, work in tr.
Row 20 Using B, work in dc.
Row 21 Using B, work in tr.
Row 22 Using D, work in tr.
Rows 23, 24, 25 and 26 Using C, work in tr.
Row 27 Using C, work in dc.
Row 28 Using E, work in dc.
Row 29 Using E, work in tr.
Row 30 Using C, work in dc.
Row 31 Using A, work in tr.
Row 32 Using A, work in dc.
Rows 33, 34 and 35 Using C, work in tr.
Row 36 Using B, work in tr.
Rows 37 and 38 Using D, work in tr.
Row 39 Using F, work in tr.
Rows 40 and 41 Using D, work in tr.
Row 42 Using C, work in tr.
Rows 43 and 44 Using D, work in tr.
Row 45 Using C, work in dc.
Rows 46 and 47 Using D, work in tr.
Fasten off.

To make Stripe 2 cushion front

Foundation chain Using a 3.5mm hook and B, make 70 chain.
Row 1 1 tr in 4th ch from hook, 1 tr in each of remaining ch to end, turn. *68 sts.*
Row 2 Using G, 3 ch (counts as first tr), miss first tr in row below, *1 tr in next tr; rep from * to end, then work last tr in top of 3-ch at end, turn.
Row 3 Using G, 1 ch (does NOT count as a stitch), 1 dc in each tr to end, then work last dc in top of 3-ch at end, turn. *68 sts.*
Row 4 Using D, 3 ch (counts as first tr), miss first dc in row below, *1 tr in next dc; rep from * to end, turn. *68 sts.*
Row 5 Using D, work in dc (when working dc into a tr row, work as row 3).
Row 6 Using H, work in tr (when working tr into a dc row, work as row 4).
Row 7 Using B, work in tr.
Row 8 Using B, work in dc.
Row 9 Using A, work in tr.
Row 10 Using A, work in dc.
Row 11 Using B, work in tr.
Rows 12 and 13 Using F, work in tr.
Row 14 Using B, work in dc.
Row 15 Using C, work in tr.
Rows 16 and 17 Using B, work in tr.
Row 18 Using J, work in tr.

One chain is worked at the beginning of each row of double crochet but this does NOT count as a stitch; three chains are worked at the beginning of each row of treble crochet and this DOES count as a stitch. Count your stitches frequently to make sure you always have 68 stitches in each row.

To make Stripe 1 cushion front

Foundation chain Using a 3.5mm hook and A, make 70 chain.
Row 1 1 tr in 4th ch from hook, 1 tr in each of remaining ch to end, turn. *68 sts.*
Row 2 3 ch (counts as first tr), miss first tr in row below, *1 tr in next tr; rep from * to end, then work last tr in top of 3-ch at end, turn.
Rows 3 and 4 Using B, [repeat row 2] twice.
Row 5 Using B, 1 ch (does NOT count as a stitch), 1 dc in each tr to end, then work last dc in top of 3-ch at end, turn. *68 sts.*
Row 6 Using C, 1 ch (does NOT count as a stitch), 1 dc in each dc to end, turn.
Row 7 Using B, 3 ch (counts as first tr), miss first dc in row below, *1 tr in next dc; rep from * to end, turn. *68 sts.*
Row 8 Using C, work in dc (when working dc into a tr row, work as row 5).
Row 9 Using D, work in tr (when working tr into a dc row, work as row 7).
Row 10 Using C, work in dc (as row 5).
Rows 11, 12 and 13 Using D, work in tr.
Row 14 Using D, work in dc.

Rows **19 and 20** Using E, work in tr.
Row **21** Using E, work in dc.
Rows **22 and 23** Using C, work in tr.
Row **24** Using B, work in tr.
Row **25** Using G, work in tr.
Row **26** Using D, work in tr.
Row **27** Using G, work in tr.
Row **28** Using A, work in tr.
Row **29** Using A, work in dc.
Row **30** Using F, work in tr.
Row **31** Using F, work in dc.
Row **32** Using B, work in tr.
Row **33** Using H, work in dc.
Row **34** Using H, work in tr.
Row **35** Using D, work in tr.
Row **36** Using A, work in tr.
Row **37** Using A, work in dc.
Rows **38 and 39** Using B, work in tr.
Row **40** Using J, work in tr.
Rows **41 and 42** Using G, work in tr.

Row **43** Using G, work in dc.
Row **44** Using D, work in tr.
Rows **45 and 46** Using E, work in tr.
Row **47** Using D, work in tr.
Fasten off.

To finish cushions
Weave in any loose ends.
Lay work out flat and gently steam on wrong side.
Fabric cushion back
Press 1.5cm to wrong side all around edge of fabric piece for cushion back, so it is same size as crocheted front. Then tack this hem in place. Pin crochet piece to wrong side of fabric, easing to fit if necessary. Tack in place through all layers around three sides. Using sewing thread, sew fabric back to front, leaving one side open. Remove tacking.
Insert cushion pad. Sew remaining side closed.

Masterclass

Joining in new colours
You can work narrow stripes without breaking off the yarn when you change from one colour to another. This means that you have less yarn ends to sew in once you have finished the piece. In order to do this, the stripes have to consist of an even number of rows so you are always beginning and ending a colour on the same side of the work.

1 In the row before the new stripe colour is to be joined in, work to the last stitch, then work the last stitch up to the point when there is one more 'yrh' left to complete the stitch.

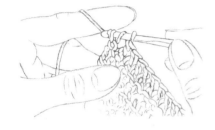

2 Drop the working yarn and wrap the new yarn around the hook and draw it through the remaining loops to complete the stitch.

3 Continue working the turning chain and the subsequent row in the new colour. Leave a long enough tail so you can thread the yarn onto a blunt-ended needle and weave it in when you have finished the piece.

Laptop cover

This simple cover for a 33cm-wide laptop is worked in robust parcel string using double crochet and introduces the techniques of increasing and decreasing. It is finished with a bright colour zip.

Skill level

EASY

In this project you will learn
Practising double crochet
Working with unusual yarn textures
Increasing
Decreasing
Working a double crochet seam

Stitches used
Double crochet

Size
Approximately 35cm x 25.5cm

Materials
4 x 90m balls of fine, soft parcel string
3mm and 3.5mm crochet hooks
50cm bright pink plastic zip and matching sewing
   thread

Tension
17½ stitches and 21 rows to 10cm measured over double crochet using a 3.5mm hook.

Abbreviations
See page 45.

To make cover front
Foundation chain Using a 3.5mm hook and string, make 50 chain.
Row 1 1 dc in 2nd ch from hook, 1 dc in each of remaining ch to end, turn. *49 sts.*
Row 2 (inc row) 1 ch (does NOT count as a stitch), 2 dc in first dc, 1 dc in each dc to last dc, 2 dc in last dc, turn. *51 sts.* (*2 sts increased*—one at each end of row.)
Repeat row 2 five times more. *61 sts.*
Next row 1 ch (does NOT count as a stitch), 1 dc in each dc to end, turn.
Repeat last row until work measures 22cm from beginning.
Next row (dec row) 1 ch (does NOT count as a stitch), insert hook in first dc, yrh and draw a loop through, insert hook in next dc, yrh and draw a loop through, yrh and draw through all 3 loops on hook, 1 dc in each dc to last 2 dc, [insert hook in next dc, yrh and draw a loop through] twice, yrh and draw through all 3 loops on hook, turn. *59 sts.* (*2 sts decreased*—one at each end of row.)
Repeat last row five times more. *49 sts.*
Next row 1 ch (does NOT count as a stitch), 1 dc in each dc to end.
Fasten off.

To make cover back
Make exactly as for front.

To finish
Weave in any loose ends.
Lay work out flat and gently steam on wrong side.

Double crochet seam
Place the the front piece on top of the back piece. Then using a 3mm hook and string, work dc evenly along the edge through both layers, leaving a 50cm opening at one end of the case. (This seam remains on the outside of the case.)

Zip opening
The zip is sewn to the outside of the case to form a decorative border along the outer edge of the opening on the front and back of the case.

To do this, fold the zip in half lengthways with wrong sides together, then position the wrong side of one zip tape on the right side of the front of the case along the opening, and the wrong side of the other zip tape on the right side of the back of the case.
Pin, then tack the zip in place.
Sew the zip tape to the case along the outer edge of both zip tapes, using small overcast stitches. Remove the tacking.

Masterclass

Increasing at the start of the row

1 Make a turning chain of the appropriate height – the laptop cover is worked in double crochet, so here it is one chain. Work a double crochet into the first stitch.

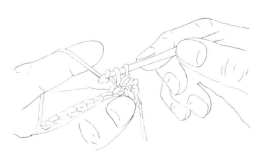

2 Work another double crochet into the same stitch to increase by one stitch. Continue to the end of the row. (For a smoother edge, you can work the extra stitch into the second stitch instead of the first.)

Increasing at the end of the row

1 Work to the last stitch in the row and work a double crochet into this stitch.

2 Work another double crochet into the same stitch to increase by one stitch. (For a smoother edge, work the extra stitch into the second to last stitch instead of the last.)

Texture throw

I loved the blankets that were always folded on the bottom of the bed at my granny's, just in case it got chilly in the night. Inspired by that memory, I have given this simple throw a more contemporary look worked in British sheep breeds wool in a natural, neutral colour. The chunky weight yarn gives an authentic country – but more luxurious – take on this classic. It is crocheted in easy rope stitch with a half-treble border, which gives a lovely contrast.

Skill level

EASY

In this project you will learn

A new stitch, called rope stitch
Working on a large scale
Adding an edging
Practising half treble crochet

Stitches used

Rope stitch, using treble crochet and chains
Half treble crochet

Size

Approximately 134cm x 154cm

Materials

Rowan Purelife British Sheep Breeds Chunky Undyed, a chunky-weight wool yarn, in one colour:

> 16 x 100g balls in light grey (954 Steel Grey Suffolk)

7mm and 8mm crochet hooks

Tension

3½ V-stitches and 5 rows to 10cm measured over rope stitch pattern using an 8mm hook. 10½ htr and 9 rows to 10cm measured over simple htr edging stitch pattern using a 7mm hook.

Abbreviations

See page 45.

Special pattern note

To work a tension swatch in rope stitch, make a multiple of 3 chains for the foundation chain – 18 chain will be sufficient. Using an 8mm hook, work rows 1 and 2 of the pattern, then repeat row 2 until the swatch measures approximately 13cm long. This will create a swatch big enough to test your tension.

To make throw

Foundation chain Using an 8mm hook, make 129 chain.
Begin the rope stitch pattern as follows:
Row 1 1 tr in 4th chain from hook, 1 ch, 1 tr in next ch, *miss 1 ch, 1 tr in next ch, 1 ch, 1 tr in next ch; rep from * to last ch, 1 tr in last ch at end, turn.
Row 2 3 ch, work [1 tr, 1 ch, 1 tr] all in each 1-ch sp to end of row, 1 tr in top of 3-ch at end, turn. *42-V stitches.*
Repeat row 2 to form the rope stitch pattern and continue in rope stitch until work measures 140cm from beginning (approximately 70 rows in total).
Fasten off.

To finish

The simple htr edging stitch is worked in rounds all around the outside edge of the throw.

Edging

Using a 7mm hook, join yarn to edge of throw with a slip stitch by inserting hook through a chain near the centre of the foundation-chain edge of the throw and drawing a loop through, then work the border in rounds as follows:

Round 1 2 ch, 1 htr in same place as slip stitch, 1 htr in next ch, then continue in htr around throw, working 1 htr in each foundation chain, 2 htr in each row end along the sides (into either the space below the tr or the space formed by the 3-ch turning chain), 1 htr in each stitch across the last row and 3 htr in each corner, join with a slip stitch to top of first htr.

Note: Do not turn at end of rounds but continue with the same side of throw always facing.

Round 2 2 ch, 1 htr in same place as slip stitch, then continue in htr around throw, working 1 htr in each htr and 3 htr in centre htr of each 3-htr group at each of 4 corners, join with a slip stitch to top of first htr of round.

Rounds 3, 4, 5 and 6 [Repeat round 2] 4 times more – border measures approximately 7cm.

Fasten off.

Weave in any loose ends.

Stitch diagram Rope Stitch

KEY

O = chain stitch

⊤ = treble crochet

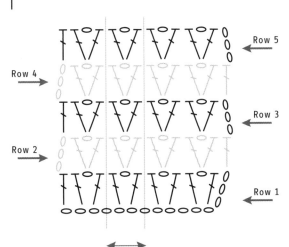

Row 5
Row 4
Row 3
Row 2
Row 1

Repeat as many
times as necessary

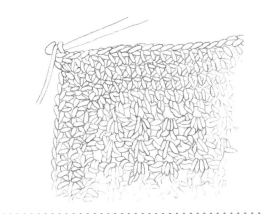

Contemporary clutch

A crocheted strip, consisting of a combination of treble crochet bobbles and shells, forms the decorative fabric of this simple clutch bag. Fastened with a plain zipper, the straight lines enhance the contemporary feel of this fold-over bag, but also makes it the perfect practice piece as no shaping is required. The contrasting vibrant orange lining creates the perfect backdrop for the neutral yarn to showcase the 'thistle pattern'.

Skill level

EASY

In this project you will learn
Making bobbles
Working shells

Stitches used
Treble crochet
Treble crochet bobbles
Treble crochet shells

Size
Approximately 25cm wide x 15–17cm deep when folded

Materials
Rowan Savannah, an aran-weight cotton-and-silk-mix yarn, in one colour:
     4 x 50g balls in beige (931 Bare)
6mm crochet hook
25cm contrasting zip and matching sewing thread
50cm lining fabric in same colour as zip

Tension
3 shells and 5 rows to 10cm measured over thistle pattern using a 6mm hook and yarn double.

Abbreviations
1 bobble = [yrh and insert hook in next st, yrh and draw a loop through, yrh and draw through first 2 loops on hook] 3 times all in same st, yrh and draw a loop through all 4 loops on hook. See also page 45.

Special notes
Use two strands of yarn held together throughout. To work a tension swatch in the thistle pattern, make a multiple of 4 chain, plus 3 chain extra, for the foundation chain – 19 chain will be sufficient. Using a 6mm hook and two strands of yarn held together, work rows 1–3 of the pattern, then repeat rows 2 and 3 until the swatch measures approximately 13cm long. This will create a swatch big enough to test your tension.

To finish

Weave in any loose ends.

Lay work out flat and gently steam on wrong side.
Cut lining fabric to same size as crochet piece, but allowing 1.5cm extra all around for hem. Fold under hem along edges of lining and pin to wrong side of crochet so fold is about 5mm from the edge of the piece along all four sides. Using matching sewing thread, stitch lining in place.
Fold piece in half widthways with right sides together and stitch side seams, using yarn.
Turn bag right side out and sew zip across the opening to right side of bag, using matching sewing thread. Fold bag in half again.

To make bag

Foundation chain Using a 6mm hook and yarn double, make 31 chain.

Row 1 (RS) 1 tr in 4th ch from hook, 1 tr in each of next 2 ch, *2 ch, miss 1 ch, 1 tr in each of next 3 ch; rep from * to last ch, 1 tr in last ch, turn.

Row 2 3 ch (counts as first tr), miss first 2 tr, work [1 bobble, 3 ch, 1 bobble] all in next tr, *miss next [1 tr, 2-ch sp, 1 tr], work [1 bobble, 3 ch, 1 bobble] all in next tr; rep from * to last tr, miss last tr and work 1 tr in top of 3-ch at end, turn.

Row 3 3 ch, 3 tr in first 3-ch arch (these 3 tr form the first 3-tr shell), *2 ch, 3 tr in next 3-ch arch; rep from * to end, 1 tr in top of 3-ch at end, turn.

Repeat rows 2 and 3 to form thistle pattern and continue in pattern until work measures 60cm. Fasten off.

Stitch diagram Thistle Pattern

KEY

o = chain stitch

┬ = treble crochet

◇ = bobble

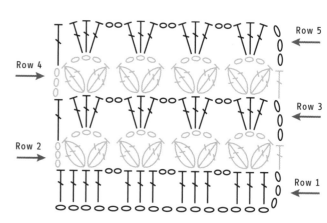

Masterclass

Working a treble bobble

A bobble is created by a raised cluster of stitches that sit on the surface of the crochet. All the stitches that make up the bobble are worked up to their last loop into the same place and then pulled together with a chain at the top of the stitch.

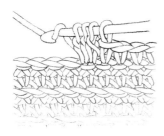

1 With the wrong side facing, work to where a bobble is required. Work 3 incomplete treble crochets, leaving the last loop of each stitch on the hook, so 4 loops remain.

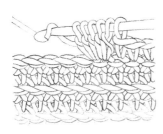

2 Work 2 more incomplete treble crochets, to leave 6 loops on the hook. Wrap the yarn around the hook and draw through all the loops on the hook.

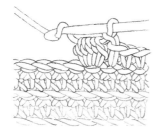

3 Wrap the yarn around the hook one last time and draw through the loop on the hook. Gently push the group of stitches through to the right side of the work.

Working a treble shell

A shell, or a fan, is usually made up of several of the same type of stitch worked into one place to create a shell-like effect. Normally all the constitutent stitches of the shell are worked into a single stitch, rather than a chain space. This helps to hold the base of the shell together, leaving the upper ends of the stitches to fan out.

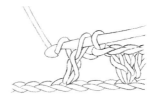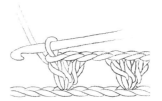

1 Work to where the shell is required, miss the number of chains/stitches as stated in the pattern (here miss 3 chain). Work a stitch into the next chain/stitch.

2 Work another 2 stitches into the same chain/stitch, thus completing one shell.

Working a treble half shell at the end of a row

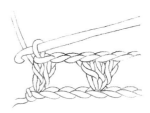

3 In order to keep the stitch count correct it may be necessary to work a half shell at the beginning or end of the row. To do this at the beginning of the row, work 2 stitches into the first stitch.

4 To do this at the end of the row, work 2 stitches into the final stitch of the row.

Fingerless mittens

Fashionably stylish and practical
fingerless mittens worked in a
decorative crochet stitch in cosy
baby alpaca yarn. The thumb holes
are created simply by skipping a few
stitches in a row, that's all.

Skill level

INTERMEDIATE

In this project you will learn
Practising half treble crochet
Working a horizontal thumb hole
Working pattern repeats

Stitches used
Half treble crochet; Treble crochet
Treble crochet bobbles

Size
One size to fit average-size woman's hand –
finished length 38cm

Materials
Rowan Baby Alpaca DK, a light double-knitting-
   weight alpaca yarn, in one colour:
       4 x 50g balls in light grey (208 Southdown)
3.5mm and 4mm crochet hooks

Tension
8 bobbles and 11 rows to 10cm measured over
zigzag lozenge stitch using a 4mm hook.

Abbreviations
1 bobble = [yrh and insert hook in 1-ch sp, yrh
and draw a loop through, yrh and draw through
first 2 loops on hook] 3 times all in same 1-ch sp,
yrh and draw a loop through all 4 loops on hook.
1 half bobble = [yrh and insert hook in 1-ch
sp, yrh and draw a loop through, yrh and draw
through first 2 loops on hook] twice all in same
1-ch sp, yrh and draw a loop through all 3 loops
on hook. See also page 45.

To make mittens
Foundation chain Using a 4mm hook, make 37
chain loosely.
Work a border of 2 rows of half treble crochet
as follows:
Row 1 1 htr in 3rd ch from hook, 1 htr in each
of remaining ch to end, turn.
Row 2 2 ch (counts as first htr), miss first htr,
*1 htr in next htr; rep from * to end, then work
last htr in top of 2-ch at end, turn. *36 sts.*
Continue in zigzag lozenge stitch as follows:
Patt row 1 (WS) 2 ch (counts as first htr), 1 htr
in first htr, *miss 1 htr, work [1 htr, 1 ch, 1 htr]
all in next htr; rep from * to last 2 htr, miss 1
htr, 2 htr in last htr, turn.
Patt row 2 (RS) 3 ch, 1 tr in first htr (counts
as a half bobble), *1 ch, 1 bobble in next 1-ch
sp; rep from * to end, 1 ch, 1 half bobble in top
of 2-ch at end of row, turn. *16 bobbles and 2
half bobbles.*
Patt row 3 2 ch (counts as first htr), *work [1 htr,
1 ch, 1 htr] all in next 1-ch sp; rep from * to end,
1 htr in top of 3-ch at end of row, turn.
Patt row 4 3 ch (counts as first tr), *1 bobble
in next 1-ch sp, 1 ch; rep from * to last 1-ch sp,
1 bobble in last sp, 1 tr in top of 2-ch at end of
row, turn. *17 bobbles.*
Patt row 5 2 ch (counts as first htr), 1 htr in first
tr, *work [1 htr, 1 ch, 1 htr] all in next 1-ch sp;
rep from * to end, 2 htr in top of 3-ch at end of
row, turn.
[Repeat patt rows 2–5] 4 times more.
Change to a 3.5mm hook and [repeat patt rows
2–5] 3 times more, so ending with a WS row.
Mitten should now measure approximately 32cm
from beginning.

Masterclass

Working a horizontal thumb hole or buttonhole

The simplest way to work an opening, whether it is for a thumb hole or buttonhole, is to miss a number of stitches in a row. At the position at which the hole is required, work a number of chain stitches that will accommodate the thumb or the diameter of the button (for these mittens, work 6 chain). Miss the number of stitches for which you have worked chain, then continue in the pattern. On the next row, work over the chain, making the same number of stitches as there are chain.

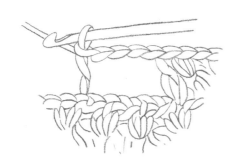

Work thumb hole

Next row (RS) 3 ch, 1 tr in first htr, *1 ch, 1 bobble in next 1-ch sp; rep from * 6 times more; 6 ch, miss next 2 1-ch sps, 1 bobble in next ch sp, **1 ch, 1 bobble in next ch sp; rep from ** to end, 1 ch, 1 half bobble in top of 2-ch at end of row, turn.

Next row 2 ch, *work [1 htr, 1 ch, 1 htr] all in next 1-ch sp; rep from * 6 times more; [1 htr, 1 ch, 1 htr] twice in 6-ch sp, **work [1 htr, 1 ch, 1 htr] all in next 1-ch sp; rep from ** to end, 1 htr in top of 3-ch at end of row, turn.

Next row Rep patt row 4. *16 bobbles.*

Next row Rep patt row 5.

Next row Rep patt row 2. *15 bobbles and 2 half bobbles.*

Next row Rep patt row 3. Fasten off.

Work second mitten in exactly the same way.

To finish

Weave in any loose ends. Gently steam on wrong side. Sew side seams.

Stitch diagrams Zigzag Lozenge Stitch

KEY

○ = chain stitch

⊤ = half treble crochet

⊥ = treble crochet

⬥ = bobble

⬦ = half bobble

Beginning of mittens

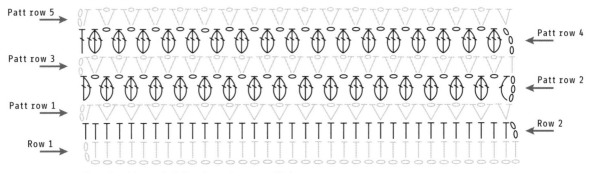

Repeat patt rows 2–5 for zigzag lozenge stitch

Thumb opening

Classic snood

A simple, luxurious and now classic snood designed to be worn around the neck in two or three loops. Worked in lace clusters, this crocheted textile has a bubbly texture of thick puffs combined with openwork V-stitches.

Skill level

INTERMEDIATE

In this project you will learn
Practising treble crochet
A new stitch, called puff stitch

Stitches used
Treble crochet
Puff stitch

Size
Approximately 25cm x 127cm

Materials
Rowan Lima, an aran-weight alpaca-mix yarn,
   in one colour:
     5 x 50g balls in pale beige (889 Peru)
5mm crochet hook

Tension
3 stitch groups (each stitch group is made up of –
1 puff stitch, 1 ch, 1 tr, 2 ch, 1 tr of pattern) and
9 rows to 10cm measured over lace puff stitch
using a 5mm hook.

Abbreviations
1 puff stitch = [yrh, insert hook in stitch and draw a long loop through] 4 times in same stitch, yrh and draw a loop through all 9 loops on hook. See also page 45.

Stitch diagram
See page 54 for the symbol diagram for the lace puff stitch.

Special pattern note
To work a tension swatch in the lace puff stitch, make a multiple of 6 chain, plus 5 chain extra, for the foundation chain – 29 chain will be sufficient. Using a 5mm hook, work rows 1–3 of the pattern, then repeat rows 2 and 3 until the swatch measures approximately 13cm long. This will create a swatch big enough to test your tension.

To make snood
Foundation chain Using a 5mm hook, make 47 chain.
Row 1 Work [1 tr, 2 ch, 1 tr] all in 4th chain from hook, *miss 2 ch, 1 puff stitch in next ch, 1 ch (this chain closes the puff stitch), miss 2 ch, work [1 tr, 2 ch, 1 tr] all in next ch; rep from * to last ch, 1 tr in last ch, turn.
Row 2 3 ch, 1 puff stitch in first 2-ch sp (between 2 tr), 1 ch, *work [1 tr, 2 ch, 1 tr] all in top of next puff stitch (under loop that closes the puff stitch), 1 puff stitch in next 2-ch sp, 1 ch; rep from * to end, 1 tr in 3-ch sp at end of row, turn.
Row 3 3 ch, work [1 tr, 2 ch, 1 tr] all in top of first puff stitch, *1 puff stitch in next 2-ch sp, 1 ch, work [1 tr, 2 ch, 1 tr] all in top of next puff stitch; rep from * to end, 1 tr in 3-ch sp at end of row, turn.
Repeat rows 2 and 3 to form the lace puff stitch and continue in pattern until work measures 127cm.
Fasten off.

To finish
Weave in any loose ends.
Twist the snood once in the middle of the length and sew the ends together.

Masterclass

The stitch pattern used to great decorative effect in this snood is made by working a combination of puff stitches and openwork V-stitches.

Working puff stitch

There are various ways of working puff stitches but they all add raised texture to otherwise flat surfaces.

1 Work 3 chain, then wrap the yarn round the hook.

2 Insert the hook into the next stitch and draw the loop through.

3 Repeat this three more times so there are nine loops on the hook.

4 Wrap the yarn round the hook and draw through all nine loops on the hook. Work one chain to close and complete the puff stitch.

Working openwork V-stitches

5 Work 1 treble into the top of the completed puff stitch in the row below, then work 2 chain.

6 Work a further 1 treble into the top of the same puff stitch.

7 Continue working alternate puff stitches and V-stitches to the last puff stitch in the row.

8 Work 1 treble into the turning chain space, turn.

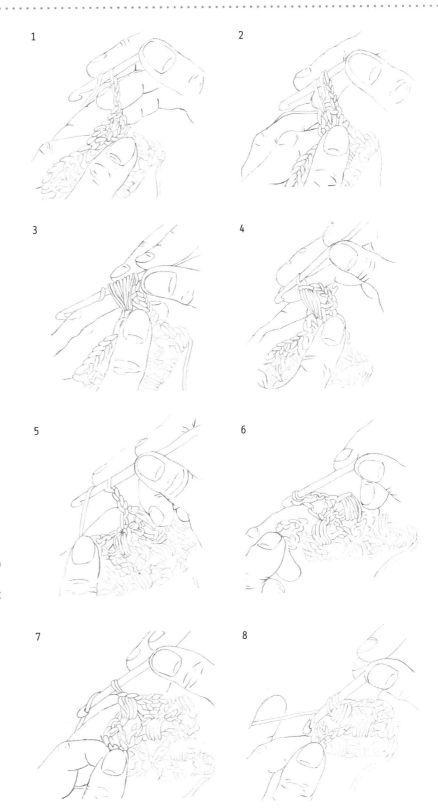

Triangular scarf

The intricate appearance of the lace stitches that make up this elegant scarf belies the simplicity of the pattern. With incremental decreases worked block by block, the scarf takes on a gently stepped triangular shape. I have used a very fine laceweight yarn in a deep plum shade to complement the filigree openwork stitches.

Skill level

INTERMEDIATE

In this project you will learn

Decreasing on a stitch pattern to form a triangle
Working with a laceweight yarn

Stitches used

Double crochet
Treble crochet

Size

Approximately 154cm across the widest part x 79cm from centre of foundation-chain edge to tip of triangle

Materials

Rowan Fine Lace, a lace-weight alpaca and wool yarn, in one colour:
      2 x 50g balls in deep plum (Era 927)
4mm and 5mm crochet hooks

Tension

$3\frac{1}{2}$ stitch repeats and 16 rows to 10cm measured over pattern using a 4mm hook.

Abbreviations

See page 45.

Special note

The starburst pattern is worked over a multiple of 6 foundation chains, plus 3 extra. If you are changing the size of the triangle, be sure to start with an odd number of stitch repeats (an odd number of 6-chain groups) so that at the finish of the decreasing you are left with one repeat at the centre.

To make scarf triangle

The scarf is begun along the longest edge and decreased gradually at each side edge to form a triangle.
Foundation chain Using a 5mm hook, make 285 chain loosely.
Change to a 4mm hook and continue in starburst pattern as follows:
Row 1 (RS) 1 dc in 2nd ch from hook, 1 dc in next ch, *6 ch, miss 4 ch, 1 dc in each of next 2 ch; rep from * to end, turn.
Row 2 3 ch (counts as first tr), miss first dc, 1 tr in next dc, *2 ch, 1 dc in 6-ch arch, 2 ch, 1 tr in each of next 2 dc; rep from * to end, turn.
Row 3 3 ch, miss first tr, 1 tr in next tr, *3 ch, 1 slip stitch in next dc, 3 ch, 1 tr in each of next 2 tr; rep from * to end, working last tr of last repeat in top of 3-ch at end of row, turn.
Row 4 1 ch, 1 dc in each of first 2 tr, *4 ch, 1 dc in each of next 2 tr; rep from * to end, working last dc of last repeat in top of 3-ch at end of row, turn.
Row 5 (decrease row) Miss first dc, slip stitch across next dc and 4 ch, 1 ch, 1 dc in each of next 2 dc, *6 ch, 1 dc in each of next 2 dc; rep from * until 4-ch and 2 dc remain, turn. *2 stitch repeats decreased.*

Repeat rows 2–5 to form the scarf triangle, decreasing one stitch repeat at each end on every 4th row (every *row 5*) as set, until only one stitch repeat remains to be worked. Work rows 2–4 as set, then work the last row.
Last row 1 ch, 1 dc in each of first 2 dc, 6 ch, 1 dc in each of next 2 dc.
Fasten off.

To finish
Weave in any loose ends.
Edging
With RS of work facing and using a 4mm hook, position the starting chain near you and join yarn with a slip stitch to the first slip stitch in the 5th row from the start (on the right edge of the scarf), then work edging as follows:
Round 1 *4 ch, 1 tr in inner corner formed by decrease, 4 ch, 1 slip stitch in outer corner of next block*; rep from * to * to point of the scarf, work 4 ch, 1 tr in 6-ch sp at point, 4 ch, 1 slip stitch to outer corner of same block, then rep from * to * along other edge of scarf. Fasten off.
Lay scarf out flat and steam gently on wrong side.

Stitch diagram Starburst Pattern

KEY
- • = slip stitch
- ○ = chain stitch
- + = double crochet
- ⊤ = treble crochet

Masterclass

Traditionally crochet sought to imitate beautiful Flemish lace and initially was worked using extremely fine yarns, most especially linen or cotton. Often one can only stare in wonderment at the intricate finesse of vintage crochet pieces.

Working with laceweight yarns can seem intimidating as they appear slow and tedious to work with. However working with extremely fine yarns can create endless creative possibilities. I most especially like to crochet relatively traditional openwork stitches but with a large hook. The resulting textile is unexpected, interesting and gives a beautiful new perspective to a garment.

Gossamer-fine shawls, wraps and scarves are especially lovely to work in this experimental way and, moreover, they work up quickly when made on a large, rather than tiny, hook. Furthermore, laceweight yarn has great yardage so it really does go a long, long way making those exquisite hand-dyed laceweight yarns that are increasingly available look a little more justifiable in price.

Generally when crocheting with ultra-fine yarns – or whisper-fine, as I like to call them – I work the foundation row loosely by going up a hook size so that it creates more flexibity.

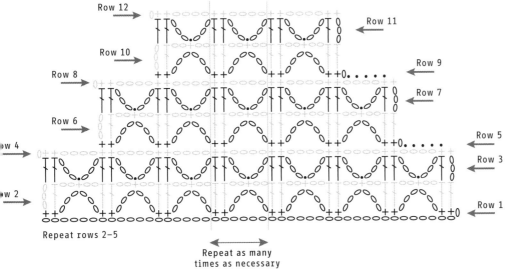

Row 12 Row 11 Row 10 Row 9 Row 8 Row 7 Row 6 Row 5 Row 4 Row 3 Row 2 Row 1

Repeat rows 2–5

Repeat as many times as necessary

Slipper boots

Crocheted in firm, dense double crochet using a robust, hardwearing British sheeps breed wool, this is my take on the ubiquitous twenty-first century footwear: the slipper boot.

Skill level

INTERMEDIATE

In this project you will learn

Working a simple double crochet decrease
Working a simple double crochet increase
Designing to fit your size

Stitches used

Double crochet

Size

Sole of this woman's slipper measures approximately 24.5cm long (to adjust size, see masterclass on page 94)

Materials

Rowan Purelife British Sheep Breeds Chunky Undyed, a chunky-weight wool yarn, in one colour:

    2 x 100g balls in light grey (954 Steel Grey Suffolk)

7mm crochet hook
Scraps of leather, or suede, and matching sewing thread

Tension

10 sts and 14 rows to 10cm measured over dc using a 7mm hook.

Abbreviations

dc2tog = [insert hook in next st, yrh and draw a loop through] twice, yrh and draw through all 3 loops on hook – one stitch decreased.
See also page 45.

To make slipper uppers (make 2)

The slippers are made in two separate pieces – the upper and the sole.

Leg
The leg is worked in rounds as follows:
Base ring Using a 7mm hook, make 31 ch and join with a slip stitch to first chain to form a ring. (Make sure that the chain is not twisted when you join the chain into a ring.)
Round 1 (WS) 1 ch, 1 dc in same place as slip stitch, 1 dc in each of remaining ch to end, join with a slip stitch to first dc. *31 dc.*
Note: Do not turn at end of rounds but continue with WS always facing.
Round 2 1 ch, 1 dc in same place as slip stitch, 1 dc in each dc to end, join with a slip stitch to first dc. *31 dc.*
Repeat last round 4 times more.

Heel
The heel is worked in rows as follows:
Row 1 (WS) 1 ch, 1 dc in same place as slip stitch, 1 dc in each dc to end, turn. *31 dc.*
Row 2 (RS) 1 ch, 1 dc in each dc to end, turn.
Row 3 1 ch, dc2tog, 1 dc in each dc to last 2 dc, dc2tog, turn. *29 dc.*
Row 4 1 ch, 1 dc in each dc to end, turn.
Row 5 1 ch, 1 dc in each dc to end, turn.

Instep
The instep is worked in rounds as follows:
Round 6 (RS) 1 ch, 1 dc in each dc to last dc, 2 dc in last dc, then work 11 dc across instep (row-end edges), join with a slip stitch to first dc.
Round 7 1 ch, 1 dc in same place as slip stitch, 1 dc in each dc to end, join with a slip stitch to first dc, turn.

Top of foot
Starting with a WS row, the foot is worked in rows as follows:
Row 8 1 ch, 1 dc in each of next 14 dc, turn. *14 dc.*
Rows 9, 10 and 11 [Rep row 8] 3 times.
Row 12 1 ch, 1 dc in each dc to last 2 dc, dc2tog, turn. *13 dc.*
Row 13 1 ch, 1 dc in each dc to last 2 dc, dc2tog, turn. *12 dc.*
Rows 14 and 15 1 ch, 1 dc in each dc to end, turn.
Row 16 1 ch, 1 dc in each dc to last 2 dc, dc2tog, turn. *11 dc.*
Row 17 1 ch, 1 dc in each dc to last 2 dc, dc2tog, turn. *10 dc.*
Row 18 1 ch, 1 dc in each dc to last 2 dc, dc2tog, turn. *9 dc.*
Row 19 1 ch, 1 dc in each dc to last 2 dc, dc2tog, turn. *8 dc.*
Fasten off and turn leg right side out.
Make second upper in exactly the same way.

To make soles (make 2)
The sole is worked from the heel to the toe.
Foundation chain Using a 7mm hook, make 5 chain.
Row 1 1 dc in 2nd ch from hook, 1 dc in each of remaining ch to end, turn. *4 dc.*
Row 2 1 ch, 1 dc in each dc to end, turn.
Row 3 1 ch, 2 dc in first dc, 1 dc in each dc to last dc, 2 dc in last dc, turn. *6 dc.*
Repeat row 2 until work measures 13.5cm from beginning.
Next row 1 ch, 2 dc in first dc, 1 dc in each dc to last dc, 2 dc in last dc, turn. *8 dc.*

Repeat row 2 until work measures 23cm from beginning.
Next row 1 ch, dc2tog, 1 dc in each dc to last 2 dc, dc2tog, turn. *6 dc.*
Next row 1 ch, dc2tog, 1 dc in each dc to last 2 dc, dc2tog, turn. *4 dc.*
Fasten off.
Make second sole in exactly the same way.

To finish
Weave in any loose ends.
Pin sole to upper with wrong sides together, easing to fit around toe. Using a 7mm hook, join yarn with a slip stitch to centre of heel, inserting hook through both layers, work 1 ch, then work dc through both layers all around, join with a slip stitch to first dc.
Fasten off and weave in end.
If desired, turn down first three rows of leg to form a 'cuff' at top of slipper.
Cut two pieces of leather for each slipper, using the two templates (see page 143), one to for the sole under the ball of the foot and one for the sole under the heel. Hand sew these leather pads to the soles, using a matching sewing thread.
Note: To make the hand sewing easier, if you have a sewing machine use it to punch holes through the leather. Set the sewing machine to an extra-long stitch and do not thread the needle, then stitch all around the cut out shapes, 4mm from the edge. Overcast stitch the pieces in place through the punched holes.

Masterclass

Adjusting the pattern for different sizes
One of crochet's greatest qualitites is its flexibility. As this slipper boot is worked in basic double crochet, it very easy to adjust the length and width of the basic shape to suit different foot sizes. If you have a narrow foot, take out 2 chain from the width of the sole and 2 stitches from the top of the foot; or alternatively if you have a wide foot, add 2 chain (and 2 stitches) to the width. Alter the length of the foot by working fewer or more rows within the straight sole (and top of foot) section. As a general tip, add or subtract 1cm if you wish to make a larger or smaller size. This is a very versatile pattern: I prefer a short boot that I wear with the edge rolled down to form a cuff but you can work a longer cuff for a higher boot and even work the initial row in a contrast yarn to give a further decorative detail.

Bejewelled brooches

An extremely easy, learn-to-crochet project for practising and perfecting work in the round. These simple round motifs are worked in jewel-colour yarns and embellished with vibrant stones and other gems to create jewellery pins. If you can't find suitable gem stones to buy, break up an inexpensive second-hand piece. I like to wear two or three of these brooches together.

Skill level

BEGINNER

In this project you will learn
Making a simple round motif

Stitches used
Double crochet
Treble crochet

Sizes
Small brooch: Approximately 3.5cm in diameter
Large brooch: Approximately 4.5cm in diameter

Materials
Small amount of Rowan Cotton Glacé or Rico
    Essentials Cotton DK, a double-knitting-weight
    cotton yarn, or a natural cotton yarn of the
    same weight, in desired colour for each brooch
4mm crochet hook
Large square- or round-shaped jewels or crystals
    with holes, or large decorative buttons
Brooch pin for each brooch
Scrap of leather or felt and matching sewing
    thread

Tension
Don't worry too much about tension for this project.

Abbreviations
See page 45.

Special yarn note
Use two strands of yarn held together throughout.

To make small brooch
Base ring Using a 4mm hook and yarn double, make 3 ch and join with a slip stitch to first ch to form a ring.
Round 1 (WS) 1 ch, 8 dc in ring, join with a slip stitch to 1-ch at beginning of round.
Note: Do not turn at end of rounds but continue with WS of brooch always facing.
Round 2 1 ch, [1 dc in next dc, 2 dc in next dc] 4 times, join with a slip stitch to 1-ch at beginning of round.
Round 3 1 ch, [insert hook through centre hole, yrh and draw a long loop through, yrh and draw a loop through 2 loops on hook] 16 times, join with a slip stitch to 1-ch at beginning of round.
Round 4 1 ch, [miss next st, 1 dc in next st] 8 times, join with a slip stitch to 1-ch at beginning of round.
Fasten off, leaving a long loose end.

To make large brooch

Base ring Using a 4mm hook and yarn double, make 3 ch and join with a slip stitch to first ch to form a ring.

Round 1 1 ch, 8 dc in ring, join with a slip stitch to 1-ch at beginning of round.

Note: Do not turn at end of rounds but continue with same side of brooch always facing.

Round 2 3 ch, [1 tr in next dc, 2 tr in next dc] 4 times, join with a slip stitch to top of 3-ch at beginning of round.

Round 3 1 ch, [insert hook through centre hole, yrh and draw a long loop through, yrh and draw a loop through 2 loops on hook] 16 times, join with a slip stitch to 1-ch at beginning of round.

Round 3 1 ch, [miss next st, 1 dc in next st] 8 times, join with a slip stitch to 1-ch at

beginning of round.
Fasten off, leaving a long loose end.

To finish

Weave in the loose end of the base ring, but leave the finishing long loose end.

Sew the selected jewel (or button) to the centre of the front of the motif.

Using the remaining long loose end, work an overcast stitch in each stitch all around the outer edge of the last round of the motif, pull to gather and secure.

Cut a small circle from the scrap of leather or felt and sew a brooch pin to the centre, using a matching sewing thread. Sew this piece to the back of the crochet motif.

Masterclass

Making a ball button

The technique I have used here to make these three-dimensional motif brooches is the same as you might use to make a crocheted ball button. By using this technique you can make a firm button simply using yarn and a hook, without the need for a plastic or metal foundation ring. You can vary the size and thickness of the motif or button depending on the weight of yarn used.

Make your ball button following the instructions for the small brooch on page 96. To begin, work the base ring and rounds 1 and 2. On round 3 work the double crochet stitches through the centre of the button as shown in step 1 below. When working round 4, you will see how decreasing stitches draws the button into a ball shape (see step 2 below). Fasten off leaving a 30cm-long loose end.

Thread the long end onto a tapestry needle. Work an overcast stitch through each outside stitch, then pull stitches together. Tie the beginning and end strands together, then sew an 'X' across the button back for attaching to the garment.

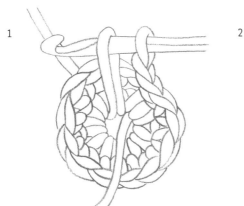

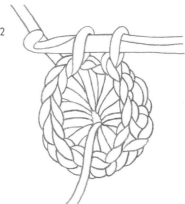

Round rug

The extreme yarn used to make this rug is an industrial waste product – the selvedges from woven wool. Putting to use this by-product of the fabric trade, I have worked in the round on an oversized hook to match the yarn's scale. Crocheting knotted fabric strips creates a similarly unique textile.

Skill level

INTERMEDIATE

In this project you will learn
Using extreme yarn and a large hook
Working a large-scale flat motif in the round
How to make yarn from fabric strips, see
   masterclass on page 102

Stitches used
Double crochet

Size
Approximately 90cm in diameter

Materials
Ingrid Wagner Big Knit Yarn, a thrum yarn
   consisting of a continuous 2.5cm-wide strip of
   patterned woven wool fabric, in five colours:
   A 1 x ball in first dark colour
   B 1 x ball in first neutral colour
   C 1 x ball in second dark colour
   D 1 x ball in second neutral colour
   E 1 x ball in third dark colour
25mm crochet hook

Tension
3 sts and 3 rows to 10cm measured over double crochet using a 25mm hook.

Abbreviations
See page 45.

Special pattern note
Mark the first chain at the beginning of every round with a coloured thread.

To make rug
Base ring Using a 25mm hook and A, make 4 chain and join with a slip stitch to first chain to form a ring.

Round 1 (RS) Using A, 1 ch (counts as first dc), 5 dc in ring, join with a slip stitch to first ch. *6 sts.*
Note: Do not turn at end of rounds but continue with RS of rug always facing.

Round 2 Using A, 1 ch (counts as first dc), 1 dc in same place as last slip stitch, *2 dc in next dc; rep from * to end of round, join with a slip stitch to first ch. *12 sts.*

Round 3 Using B, 1 ch (counts as first dc), 1 dc in same place as last slip stitch, 1 dc in next dc, *2 dc in next dc, 1 dc in next dc; rep from * to end of round, join with a slip stitch to first ch. *18 sts.*

Round 4 Using B, 1 ch (counts as first dc), 1 dc in same place as last slip stitch, 1 dc in each of next 2 dc, *2 dc in next dc, 1 dc in each of next 2 dc; rep from * to end of round, join with a slip stitch to first ch. *24 sts.*

Round 5 Using B, 1 ch (counts as first dc), 1 dc in same place as last slip stitch, 1 dc in each of next 3 dc, *2 dc in next dc, 1 dc in each of next 3 dc; rep from * to end of round, join with a slip stitch to first ch. *30 sts.*

Round 6 Using B, 1 ch (counts as first dc), 1 dc in same place as last slip stitch, 1 dc in each of next 4 dc, *2 dc in next dc, 1 dc in each of next 4 dc; rep from * to end of round, join with a slip stitch to first ch. *36 sts.*

Round 7 Using B, 1 ch (counts as first dc), 1 dc in same place as last slip stitch, 1 dc in each of next 5 dc, *2 dc in next dc, 1 dc in each of next 5 dc; rep from * to end of round, join with a slip stitch to first ch. *42 sts.*

Round 8 Using C, 1 ch (counts as first dc), 1 dc in same place as last slip stitch, 1 dc in each of next 6 dc, *2 dc in next dc, 1 dc in each of next 6 dc; rep from * to end of round, join with a slip stitch to first ch. *48 sts.*

Round 9 Using D, 1 ch (counts as first dc), 1 dc in

same place as last slip stitch, 1 dc in each of next 7 dc, *2 dc in next dc, 1 dc in each of next 7 dc; rep from * to end of round, join with a slip stitch to first ch. *54 sts.*

Round 10 Using D, 1 ch (counts as first dc), 1 dc in same place as last slip stitch, 1 dc in each of next 8 dc, *2 dc in next dc, 1 dc in each of next 8 dc; rep from * to end of round, join with a slip stitch to first ch. *60 sts.*

Round 11 Using D, 1 ch (counts as first dc), 1 dc in same place as last slip stitch, 1 dc in each of next 9 dc, *2 dc in next dc, 1 dc in each of next 9 dc; rep from * to end of round, join with a slip stitch to first ch. *66 sts.*

Round 12 Using E, 1 ch (counts as first dc), 1 dc in

same place as last slip stitch, 1 dc in each of next 10 dc, *2 dc in next dc, 1 dc in each of next 10 dc; rep from * to end of round, join with a slip stitch to first ch. *72 sts.*

Round 13 Using E, 1 ch (counts as first dc), 1 dc in same place as last slip stitch, 1 dc in each of next 11 dc, *2 dc in next dc, 1 dc in each of next 11 dc; rep from * to end of round, join with a slip stitch to first ch. *78 sts.*
Fasten off.

To finish
Weave in any loose ends.
Lay work out flat and gently steam on wrong side.

....

Masterclass

Making yarn from fabric strips
Making your own fabric yarn is as simple as cutting and knotting together fabric strips.

1 Lay each piece of fabric on a flat surface, and using sharp scissors begin to cut into strips approximately 2.5cm wide.

2 When you reach the end of the strip, stop approximately 1cm from the edge. Start cutting the next strip 2.5cm along. This creates a continuous strip of fabric.

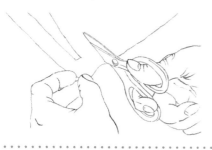

3 Cut each piece of fabric in this way to make long strips of each colour or pattern. Start to wind the first fabric strip into a ball. Join the next strip with a double knot and continue to wind into a ball. The knots will form part of the textile.

4 Work a foundation chain in the usual way, however you may need to pay closer attention to your tension as, depending on the fabric, it may or may not be a little stretchy. Do not work the chains too tightly.

Rag pet bed

With two cats and a dog sharing my home, I know you can never have too many pet beds to avoid territorial turf conflict. To maintain household harmony, I periodically make this simple project. Worked in knotted strips of complimentary fabrics using double and treble crochet, this is an inexpensive bed for your four-legged friends.

Skill level

INTERMEDIATE

In this project you will learn
Working an external decrease, see masterclass on page 106
How to create a three-dimensional shape in the round

Stitches used
Double crochet; Treble crochet

Size
Approximately 50cm in diameter x 22cm tall

Materials
Four different fabrics for making your own yarn:
2m natural linen fabric
2m black and white gingham
1m calico
2m black and white striped ticking fabric
9mm and 10mm crochet hooks
Optional – round cushion pad, 50-cm in diameter

Tension
Approximately 7 sts and 8 rows to 10cm measured over double crochet using a 10mm hook and 1.5cm-wide fabric strips.

Abbreviations
See page 45.

Special yarn strip notes
If necessary, wash the fabrics you are cutting into yarn strips first to take the 'dressing' out to aid crocheting. Alternatively, you may prefer the more solid characteristic of the dressed material. Before starting to work, cut some long 1.5cm-wide strips on the straight grain from each of the fabrics. Cut more strips as you need them. See masterclass on page 102 for tips on cutting 'yarn' strips.

To make pet bed
Start with any strip of fabric and use different fabrics at random, changing at any point by just knotting the two strips together.
Bed base
Base ring Using a 10mm hook and a 1.5cm-wide strip of fabric, make 6 ch and join with a slip stitch to first chain to form a ring.
Round 1 (RS) 3 ch (these first 3-ch count as first tr of each round), 11 tr in ring, join with a slip stitch to top of 3-ch at beginning of round. *12 sts.*
Note: Do not turn at end of rounds but continue with RS of work always facing.
Round 2 3 ch, 1 tr in same place as last slip stitch, *2 tr in next tr; rep from * to end of round, join with a slip stitch to top of 3-ch at beginning of round. *24 sts.*
Round 3 3 ch, 1 tr in same place as last slip stitch, 1 tr in next tr, *2 tr in next tr, 1 tr in next tr; rep from * to end, join with a slip stitch to top of 3-ch. *36 sts.*
Round 4 3 ch, 1 tr in same place as last slip stitch, 1 tr in each of next 2 tr, *2 tr in next tr, 1 tr in each of next 2 tr; rep from * to end, join with a slip stitch to top of 3-ch. *48 sts.*
Round 5 3 ch, 1 tr in same place as last slip stitch, 1 tr in each of next 3 tr, *2 tr in next tr, 1 tr in each of next 3 tr; rep from * to end, join with a slip stitch to top of 3-ch. *60 sts.*
Round 6 3 ch, 1 tr in same place as last slip stitch, 1 tr in each of next 4 tr, *2 tr in next tr, 1 tr in each of next 4 tr; rep from * to end, join with a slip stitch to top of 3-ch. *72 sts.*
Round 7 3 ch, 1 tr in same place as last slip stitch, 1 tr in each of next 5 tr, *2 tr in next tr,

1 tr in each of next 5 tr; rep from * to end, join with a slip stitch to top of 3-ch. *84 sts.*

Round 8 3 ch, 1 tr in same place as last slip stitch, 1 tr in each of next 6 tr, *2 tr in next tr, 1 tr in each of next 6 tr; rep from * to end, join with a slip stitch to top of 3-ch. *96 sts.*

Round 9 3 ch, 1 tr in same place as last slip stitch, 1 tr in each of next 7 tr, *2 tr in next tr, 1 tr into each of next 7 tr; rep from * to end, join with a slip stitch to top of 3-ch. *108 sts.*

This completes the round base of the pet bed.

Begin sides of bed

The sides of the pet bed are worked in double crochet as follows:

Round 10 1 ch, 1 dc in same place as last slip stitch, 1 dc in each tr to end of round, join with a slip stitch to first dc.

Round 11 1 ch, 1 dc in same place as last slip stitch, 1 dc in each dc to end of round, join with a slip stitch to first dc.

Repeat last round until side measures 12.5cm.

Shape sides

The rest of the pet bed is worked in rows to shape the front.

Place a marker on the 1-ch at the beg of dc section of every row as it helps you to see the start and finish of each row.

Next row (WS) Turn the work so the WS is facing, 1 ch, 1 slip stitch in each of first 16 dc, 1 ch (place marker), 1 dc in each dc to end, turn. *92 dc.*

Next row 1 ch, 1 slip stitch in each of first 2 dc, 1 ch (place marker), 1 dc in each dc to end, turn.

Repeat the last row 5 times more.

Fasten off.

To finish

Tidy up any loose strip ends by weaving them into the work, although I like to leave the knots as a detail.

Edging

Using a 9mm hook, join a strip with a slip stitch to a stitch at centre of back, 1 ch, 1 dc in same place as slip stitch, then work 1 dc in each st all around edge, join with a slip stitch to first dc. Fasten off.

To make optional cushion cover

This cover is made from leftover fabric.

Front

Draw a circle 53cm in diameter on a piece of paper and cut out the circle. Cut one piece of fabric using this paper pattern piece.

Back pieces

To make the paper pattern for the two back pieces, fold the paper pattern for the front in half along the diameter. Unfold, draw a line 10cm from fold and cut along this line. Cut two pieces of fabric using this pattern piece.

Make a narrow double hem along both straight edges of the back pieces.

Sewing back pieces to front

Place one back piece on top of the front piece with right sides together and the outer edges aligned. Place second back piece on the front so that it overlaps the first piece at the centre.

Pin the back pieces to the front and stitch all around leaving a 1.5cm seam allowance. Clip the curves, turn right side out and press. Insert the cushion pad.

Masterclass

Working an external decrease

This is a method for decreasing more than one stitch at an external edge, such as the sloped front edge of the pet bed.

To decrease at the beginning of the row, work a slip stitch into each of the stitches to be decreased, then work the appropriate turning chain and continue along the row. To decrease at the end of the row, simply leave the stitches to be decreased unworked, turn, then work the appropriate turning chain and continue along the row.

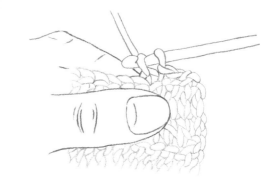

Two-colour bolster

The intricate visual effect of this two-colour 'Catherine Wheel' stitch belies the simplicity of the pattern. Only one colour is ever worked at a time, but the broken stripe design creates an interesting woven textile. The ends of this bolster are simply rounds worked into spaces and finished with a scallop edging.

Skill level

EXPERIENCED

In this project you will learn
A two-colour stitch
Working a scallop edging

Stitches used
Double crochet; Treble crochet; Double treble; Treble crochet shells; Treble crochet clusters

Size
Approximately 45cm long x 17cm in diameter

Materials
Yeoman Yarns Cotton Cannele 4-ply, a super-fine-weight mercerised cotton yarn, in two colours:
  A 1 x 250g cone in dark grey (137 Mouse)
  B 1 x 250g cone in aqua blue (147 Lagon)
3mm crochet hook
Feather bolster 45cm long x 17cm in diameter
Two 22mm dark shell buttons

Tension
28 sts and 13 rows to 10cm measured over two-colour stitch pattern using 3mm hook.

Abbreviations
1 cluster = [yrh, insert hook in next stitch, yrh and draw a loop through, yrh and draw through first 2 loops on hook] over the number of stitches indicated, yrh and draw a loop through all loops on hook to complete cluster.
See also page 45.

Special pattern note
To work a tension swatch in the two-colour stitch pattern, make a multiple of 10 chain, plus 7 chain extra, for the foundation chain – 37 chain will be sufficient. Using a 3mm hook, work rows 1–5 of the pattern, then repeat rows 2–5 until the swatch measures approximately 13cm long. This will create a swatch big enough to test your tension.

To make main part of cushion
The foundation chain and the first row of the two-colour stitch pattern (called 'Catherine Wheel' stitch) are worked in A, thereafter two rows each in B and A are repeated. When changing colour, weave in the yarn ends.
Foundation chain Using a 3mm hook and A, make 127 chain.
Row 1 (RS) Using A, 1 dc in 2nd ch from hook, 1 dc in next ch, *miss 3 ch, 7 tr in next ch (these 7 tr in same chain form a 7-tr shell), miss 3 ch, 1 dc in each of next 3 ch; rep from * to last 4 ch, miss 3 ch, 4 tr in last ch, turn.
Row 2 Using B, 1 ch, 1 dc in each of first 2 tr, *3 ch, 1 cluster over next 7 sts (that is over next 2 tr, 3 dc, 2 tr), 3 ch, 1 dc in each of next 3 tr (these 3 tr are the 3 centre sts of the 7-tr shell); rep from * to last 4 sts (remaining 2 tr and 2 dc), finishing with 3 ch, 1 cluster over these last 4 sts, turn.
Row 3 Using B, 3 ch (counts as first tr), 3 tr in top of first 4-tr cluster (under loop that closes the cluster), *miss 3-ch sp, 1 dc in each of next 3 dc, miss 3-ch sp, 7 tr in top of next cluster (under loop that closed the cluster); rep from * to last 3-ch sp, finishing with miss 3-ch sp, 1 dc in each of last 2 dc, turn.
Row 4 Using A, 3 ch (counts as first tr) miss first dc, 1 cluster over next 3 sts (that is over next 1 dc, 2 tr), *3 ch, 1 dc in each of next 3 tr (these 3 tr are the 3 centre sts of the 7-tr shell), 3 ch, 1 cluster over next 7 sts (that is over next 2 tr,

cut off the yarn not in use but leave it hanging at the back of the work to pick up for the next round.

Base ring Using a 3mm hook and A, make 4 chain and join with a slip stitch to first chain to form a ring.

Round 1 (RS) Using A, 3 ch, 2 tr in ring (counts as first 3-tr group), work [1 ch, 3 tr] 3 times in ring, 1 ch, join with a slip stitch to top of 3-ch at beginning of round. *4 3-tr groups.*

Note: Do not turn at end of rounds but continue with RS of work always facing.

Round 2 Using B, 3 ch, 2 tr in last ch sp of last round (counts as first 3-tr group), 3 tr in next tr, [3 tr in next ch sp, 3 tr in centre tr of next 3-tr group] 3 times, join with a slip stitch to top of 3-ch at beginning of round. *8 3-tr groups.*

Round 3 Using A, 3 ch, 2 tr in sp between first and last 3-tr groups of previous round (counts as first 3-tr group), 3 tr in next tr, [3 tr in each of next 2 sps (sps and sp henceforth refer to the spaces between the 3-tr groups), 3 tr in centre tr of next 3-tr group] 3 times, 3 tr in next sp, join with a slip stitch to top of 3-ch. *12 3-tr groups.*

Round 4 Using B, 3 ch, 2 tr in sp between first and last 3-tr groups, 3 tr in each of next 2 sps, [3 tr in centre tr of next 3-tr group, 3 tr in each of next 3 sps] 3 times, 3 tr in centre tr of next 3-tr group, join with a slip stitch to top of 3-ch. *16 3-tr groups.*

Round 5 Using A, 3 ch, 2 tr in sp between first and last 3-tr groups, 3 tr in next sp, [3 tr in centre tr of next 3-tr group, 3 tr in each of next 4 sps] 3 times, 3 tr in centre tr of next 3-tr group, 3 tr in each of next 2 sps, join with a slip stitch to top of 3-ch. *20 3-tr groups.*

Round 6 Using B, 3 ch, 2 tr in sp between first

3 dc, 2 tr); rep from * to last tr, finishing with 3 ch, 1 dc in last tr, 1 dc in top of 3-ch at end of row, turn.

Row 5 Using A, 1 ch, 1 dc in each of first 2 dc, *miss 3-ch sp, 7 tr in top of next cluster, miss 3-ch sp, 1 dc in each of next 3 dc; rep from * to last 3-ch sp, finishing with miss 3-ch sp, 4 tr in top of 3-ch at end of row, turn.

Repeat rows 2–5 to form two-colour stitch pattern and continue in pattern until work measures 55cm from beginning, ending with a row 4.

Fasten off.

To make cushion ends (make 2)
The cushion ends are also worked in two colours, alternating one round A and one round B. Do not

Stitch diagram Catherine Wheel Stitch

KEY

o = chain stitch

+ = double crochet

⊤ = treble crochet

= cluster

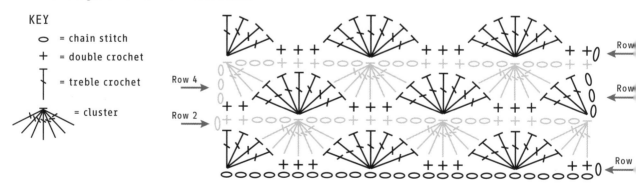

Row 4 →

Row 2 →

and last 3-tr groups, 3 tr in each of next 3 sps, [3 tr in centre tr of next 3-tr group, 3 tr in each of next 5 sps] 3 times, 3 tr in centre tr of next 3-tr group, 3 tr in next sp, join with a slip stitch to top of 3-ch. *24 3-tr groups.*

Round 7 Using A, 3 ch, 2 tr in sp between first and last 3-tr groups, 3 tr in next sp, [3 tr in centre tr of next 3-tr group, 3 tr in each of next 6 sps] 3 times, 3 tr in centre tr of next 3-tr group, 3 tr in each of next 4 sps, join with a slip stitch to top of 3-ch. *28 3-tr groups.*

Round 8 Using B, 3 ch, 2 tr in sp between first and last 3-tr groups, 3 tr in each of next 6 sps, [3 tr in centre tr of next 3-tr group, 3 tr in each of next 7 sps] 3 times, 3 tr in centre tr of next 3-tr group, join with a slip stitch to top of 3-ch. *32 3-tr groups.*

Round 9 Using A, 3 ch, 2 tr in sp between first and last 3-tr groups, 3 tr in each of next 3 sps, [3 tr in centre tr of next 3-tr group, 3 tr in each of next 8 sps] 3 times, 3 tr in centre tr of next 3-tr group, 3 tr in each of next 4 sps, join with a slip stitch to top of 3-ch. *36 3-tr groups.*

Round 10 Using B, 3 ch, 2 tr in sp between first and last 3-tr groups, 3 tr in each of next 5 sps, [3 tr in centre tr of next 3-tr group, 3 tr in each of next 9 sps] 3 times, 3 tr in centre tr of next 3-tr group, 3 tr in each of next 3 sps, join with a slip stitch to top of 3-ch. *40 3-tr groups.*
Fasten off.

Edging
With RS of work facing and using a 3mm hook and B, join yarn with a slip stitch to any stitch on the edge of the end piece and work as follows:
Miss next 2 sts, work [2 tr, 1 ch, 1 dtr, 1 ch, 2 tr] all in next st, *miss next 2 sts, 1 slip stitch in next st, miss next 2 sts, work [2 tr, 1 ch, 1 dtr, 1 ch, 2 tr] all in next st; rep from * to end, join with a slip stitch to first slip stitch.
Fasten off.
Make second end piece in exactly the same way.

To finish
Weave in any loose ends.
Lay work out flat and gently steam on wrong side.
Sew together the first and last rows of main piece.
Sew on one end all around, keeping edging free and on the outside of the bolster cover. Insert the feather bolster and sew on the second end as before.
Sew one button to centre of each end.

Masterclass

Working a scallop edging
Adding a crochet border lends a final decorative touch; it can be worked not only on a piece of crochet but also knitting and even woven fabric. To work this shell edging you need a foundation row to work into. If your piece does not already have a suitable foundation row, make a row or round of double crochet. When crocheting this border, take care to ensure that the right side of the shell edging ends up facing the correct way.

1 Ensure that the foundation row is a multiple of 6 stitches. Join the yarn to the edge with a slip stitch, miss 2 stitches, then *work 2 treble crochet, 1 chain, 1 double treble, 1 chain, 2 treble crochet into the next stitch.

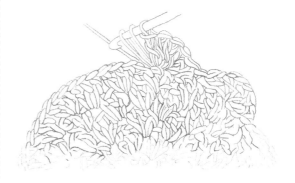

2 Miss 2 stitches, 1 slip stitch in next stitch, miss 2 stitches. Continue by repeating from * to end of the round or row. When the edging is complete, join with a slip stitch to the first slip stitch.

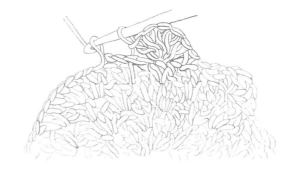

Granny Square throw

At the heart of this throw lie two traditional square motifs. Known as a 'granny square', this motif is a necessary basic that every new crocheter should master. Oversewing two of these square motifs together gives the rectangular centre around which the remaining rounds of the throw are worked. And the result? A throw that is the perfect dimensions for either a bed or sofa.

Skill level

INTERMEDIATE

In this project you will learn
Making a simple square motif

Stitches used
Treble crochet

Size
Approximately 111.5cm wide x 121cm long

Materials
Rowan Cotton Glacé, a fine-weight cotton yarn, in 11 colours:

- A 3 x 50g balls in olive (739 Dijon)
- B 2 x 50g balls in wine red (805 Burgundy)
- C 3 x 50g balls in brown (843 Toffee)
- D 1 x 50g balls in dusty lilac (828 Heather)
- E 3 x 50g balls in light brown (838 Umber)
- F 1 x 50g balls in grape (841 Garnet)
- G 2 x 50g balls in pale pink (747 Candy Floss)
- H 2 x 50g balls in medium pink (724 Bubbles)
- J 3 x 50g balls in dark mauve (806 Delight)
- K 2 x 50g balls in dark grey (808 Mystic)
- L 2 x 50g balls in blue-green (829 Twilight)

2.5mm and 3mm crochet hooks

Tension
One basic granny square measures 9.5cm x 9.5cm using a 3mm hook.

5 3-tr groups and 9½ rows to 10cm measured over main pattern using 3mm hook.

Abbreviations
See page 45.

Stitch diagram
See page 57 for the symbol diagram for the square motif.

To make throw
The centre of the throw is worked first and is made up of two basic square motifs stitched together side by side, then the main throw is worked around this rectangular centre.

Basic square motifs (make 2)
Base ring Using 3mm hook and A, make 6 ch and join with a slip stitch to first chain to form a ring.
Round 1 (RS) Using A, 3 ch (counts as first tr), 2 tr in ring, [3 ch, 3 tr in ring] 3 times, 3 ch, join with a slip stitch to top of 3-ch at beginning of round. Fasten off.
Round 2 Using B, join yarn with a slip stitch to any 3-ch sp, 3 ch (counts as first tr), [2 tr, 3 ch, 3 tr] in same 3-ch sp, *1 ch, [3 tr, 3 ch, 3 tr] in next 3-ch sp; rep from * twice more, 1 ch, join with a slip stitch to top of 3-ch at beginning of round. Fasten off.
Round 3 Using C, join yarn with a slip stitch to any 3-ch sp, 3 ch (counts as first tr), [2 tr, 3 ch, 3 tr] in same 3-ch sp, *1 ch, 3 tr in next 1-ch sp, 1 ch, [3 tr, 3 ch, 3 tr] in next 3-ch sp; rep from *

twice more, 1 ch, 3 tr in next 1-ch sp, 1 ch, join with a slip stitch to top of 3-ch at beginning of round. Fasten off.

Round 4 Using D, join on yarn with a slip stitch to any 3-ch sp, 3 ch (counts as first tr), [2 tr, 3 ch, 3 tr] in same 3-ch sp, *[1 ch, 3 tr in next 1-ch sp] twice, 1 ch, [3 tr, 3 ch, 3 tr] in next 3-ch sp; rep from * twice more, [1 ch, 3 tr in next 1-ch sp] twice, 1 ch, join with a slip stitch to top of 3-ch at beginning of round. Fasten off.

Work second basic square motif in same way, but use E for base ring and round 1, F for round 2, A for round 3 and G for round 4.

Main section

To form the rectangular throw centre, sew the two basic square motifs together along one side using neat overcast stitches.

Work the remainder of the throw around this rectangle as follows:

Round 1 (RS) With RS of work facing and using F, join on yarn with a slip stitch to a 3-ch sp at the beg of a long edge, then work 3 ch (counts as first tr), [2 tr, 3 ch, 3 tr] in same 3-ch sp, [1 ch, 3 tr in next 1-ch sp] 8 times, 1 ch, [3 tr, 3 ch, 3 tr] in next 3-ch sp, [1 ch, 3 tr in next 1-ch sp] 3 times, 1 ch, [3 tr, 3 ch, 3 tr] into next 3-ch sp, [1 ch, 3 tr in next 1-ch sp] 8 times, 1 ch, [3 tr, 3 ch, 3 tr] in next 3-ch sp, [1 ch, 3 tr in next 1-ch sp] 3 times, 1 ch, join with a slip stitch to top of 3-ch at beginning of round. Fasten off.

Round 2 Using H, join on yarn with a slip stitch to any 3-ch sp, 3 ch (counts as first tr), [2 tr, 3 ch, 3 tr] in same 3-ch sp, *[1 ch, 3 tr] in each 1-ch sp until you reach the next 3-ch corner sp, 1 ch, [3 tr, 3 ch, 3 tr] in this 3-ch sp; rep from * twice more, [1 ch, 3 tr] in each 1-ch sp to the end of the round, 1 ch, join with a slip stitch to top of 3-ch at beginning of round. Fasten off.

Repeat round 2 for 46 rounds more, changing colour each round and using the following colours: Round 3 E; round 4 J; round 5 A; round 6 E; round 7 G; round 8 K; round 9 C; round 10 B; round 11 D; round 12 F; round 13 A; round 14 L; round 15 G; round 16 E; round 17 H; round 18 J; round 19 C; round 20 K; round 21 L; round 22 H; round 23 A; round 24 F; round 25 D; round 26 A; round 27 B; round 28 E; round 29 G; round 30 J; round 31 F; round 32 L; round 33 H; round 34 C; round 35 K; round 36 B; round 37 C; round 38 G; round 39 J; round 40 A; round 41 K; round 42 E; round 43 H; round 44 J; round 45 L; round 46 A; round 47 C; round 48 J.

Fasten off.

Throw now measures approximately 110.5cm x 120cm.

To finish

Weave in any loose ends.

Edging

Using a 2.5mm hook and E, join yarn with a slip stitch to any 3-ch sp on outside edge of throw, 3 ch, [2 tr, 3 ch, 3 tr] in same 3-ch sp, then work 1 tr in each tr, 1 tr in each 1-ch sp and [3 tr, 3 ch, 3 tr] in each corner sp to end, join with a slip stitch to top of 3-ch at beginning of round.

Fasten off.

Lay work out flat and gently steam on wrong side.

Masterclass

Choosing yarns and colours for a project

The success of a crochet project more often than not hinges on the quality of the yarn selected as well as the colour palette. Traditional square motifs – or 'granny squares' – such as the ones at the centre of this throw are most often worked in wool, which gives a soft feel and a fluid textile. However, I have chosen a natural cotton yarn for this project as it gives good stitch clarity, has an attractive sheen and takes dye well so offers good clean colours. When considering a yarn, work up a large swatch and ask yourself a series of questions: Is it too heavy or too light? Is it soft to the touch? Do I like the overall effect? Whether designing garments, accessories or homewares, I lean towards an understated colour palette of muted tones. Preferring to use the characteristic colours of natural yarns as a base, I usually introduce stronger colours as highlights within the overall scheme. For this Granny Square Throw, a base of browns, greys and olive green provide a quiet backdrop for the punchier reds, pinks and plum. A zesty lime is one of my favourite accent colours to juxtapose soft ecru, fawn, brown and grey. Or for a classic colourway, team mid-blue with earthy browns. An alternative colourway comprising a range of tonal greys would be an equally chic choice for this project.

Motif tablemats 15

A simple and practical way to learn how to crochet three different round motifs. Each is made in cotton, worked in subtle, complementary neutral tones, to create a stylish, crafty and contemporary addition to the 'top of table'. A wonderfully inexpensive house gift!

Skill level

INTERMEDIATE

In this project you will learn
Working intricate motifs

Stitches used
Double crochet; Half treble crochet; Treble crochet; Double treble; Puff stitch; Treble crochet clusters

Size
Each tablemat measures approximately 20cm in diameter

Materials
Rowan Handknit Cotton, a double-knitting-weight cotton yarn, in desired colour:

> 1 x 50g ball for each tablemat motif in one of these colors – light sage green (330 Raffia), bluey lilac (334 Delphinium), ecru (205 Linen), purple (348 Aubergine), or taupe (253 Tope)

5mm crochet hook

Tension
Each finished motif measures approximately 20cm in diameter using a 5mm hook and yarn double.

Abbreviations
1 puff stitch = [yrh, insert hook in ring and draw a long loop through] twice, yrh and draw a loop through all 5 loops on hook.
1 cluster = [yrh and insert hook in next tr, yrh and draw a loop through, yrh and draw through first 2 loops on hook] 5 times, yrh and draw a

loop through all 6 loops on hook.
tr4tog = [yrh and insert hook in next tr, yrh and draw a loop through, yrh and draw through first 2 loops on hook] 4 times, yrh and draw a loop through all 5 loops on hook.
See also page 45.

Special yarn note
Use two strands of yarn held together throughout.

To make wagon wheel tablemat
This tablemat is shown worked in three different colours – light sage green (Raffia), taupe (Tope) and bluey lilac (Delphinium).
Base ring Using a 5mm hook and yarn double, make 4 chain and join with a slip stitch to first chain to form a ring.
Round 1 (RS) 3 ch and 1 htr in ring (counts as first puff st), 1 ch, [1 puff stitch, 1 ch] 7 times in ring, join with a slip stitch to top of 3-ch at beginning of round. *8 petals.*
Round 2 1 slip stitch in next htr, 1 slip stitch in next ch sp, 3 ch, 1 tr in same ch sp as last slip stitch, 2 ch, [2 tr, 2 ch] in each of next 7 ch sps, join with a slip stitch to top of 3-ch at beginning of round.
Round 3 1 slip stitch in next tr, 1 slip stitch in next ch sp, 3 ch, [1 tr, 1 ch, 2 tr] in same ch sp as last slip stitch, 1 ch, [2 tr, 1 ch] twice in each of next 7 ch sps, join with a slip stitch to top of 3-ch at beginning of round.
Round 4 1 slip stitch in next tr, 1 slip stitch in next ch sp, 3 ch, 2 tr in same ch sp as last slip stitch, 1 ch, [3 tr, 1 ch] in each of next 15 ch sps, join with a slip stitch to top of 3-ch at beginning of round.
Round 5 1 slip stitch in each of next 2 tr, 1 slip stitch in next ch sp, 3 ch, 3 tr in same ch

stitch in next ch sp, 3 ch, 3 tr in same ch sp as last slip stitch, 1 ch, [4 tr, 1 ch] in each of next 15 ch sps, join with a slip stitch to top of 3-ch at beginning of round.
Round 6 1 slip stitch in each of next 3 tr, 1 slip stitch in next ch sp, 3 ch, 3 tr in same ch sp as last slip stitch, 2 ch, [4 tr, 2 ch] in each of next 15 ch sps, join with a slip stitch to top of 3-ch at beginning of round.
Fasten off.

To make begonia wheel tablemat

This tablemat is shown worked two different colours – ecru (Linen) and bluey lilac (Delphinium).
Base ring Using a 5mm hook and yarn double, make 6 chain and join with a slip stitch to first chain to form a ring.
Round 1 (RS) 3 ch (counts as first tr), 13 tr in ring, join with a slip stitch to top of 3-ch at beginning of round.
Round 2 3 ch (counts as first tr), 2 tr in same place as last slip stitch, *1 ch, miss 1 tr, 3 tr in next tr; rep from * 5 times more, 1 ch, join with a slip stitch to top of 3-ch at beginning of round.
Round 3 1 slip stitch in next tr, 3 ch (counts as first tr), 1 tr in same tr as slip stitch, *1 ch, 2 tr in next 1-ch sp, 1 ch, miss 1 tr, 2 tr in next tr (centre tr of 3-tr group); rep from * 5 times more, 1 ch, 2 tr in next 1-ch sp, 1 ch, join with a slip stitch to top of 3-ch at beginning of round.

Round 4 [4 ch, 1 dc in next 1-ch sp] 13 times, 2 ch, 1 tr in base of first 4-ch.
Round 5 [4 ch, 1 dc in centre of next 4-ch sp] 13 times, 2 ch, 1 tr in tr at end of previous round.
Round 6 3 ch (counts as first tr), 3 tr in sp formed by tr at end of previous round, 4 tr in each of next 13 4-ch sps, join with a slip stitch to top of 3-ch at beginning of round.
Round 7 3 ch, 1 tr in same place as last slip stitch, 1 tr in each of next 3 tr, *2 tr in next tr, 1 tr in each of next 3 tr; rep from * 12 times more, join with a slip stitch to top of 3-ch at beginning of round.
Fasten off.

To make ice crystal tablemat

This tablemat is shown worked in three different colours – ecru (Linen), light sage green (Raffia) and purple (Aubergine).
Base ring Using a 5mm hook and yarn double, make 6 chain and join with a slip stitch to first chain to form a ring.
Round 1 (RS) 1 ch (does NOT count as a stitch), 12 dc in ring, join with a slip stitch to first dc. *12 dc.*
Round 2 1 ch (does NOT count as a stitch), 1 dc in same place as last slip stitch, [7 ch, miss 1 dc, 1 dc in next dc] 5 times, 3 ch, 1 dtr in top of first dc.
Round 3 3 ch, (counts as first tr), 4 tr in sp formed by dtr at end of previous round, [3 ch, 5 tr in next 7-ch sp] 5 times, 3 ch, join with a slip stitch to top of 3-ch at beginning of round.
Round 4 3 ch (counts as first tr), 1 tr in each of next 4 tr, *3 ch, 1 dc in next 3-ch sp, 3 ch,** 1 tr in each of next 5 tr; rep from * 4 more times and from * to ** again, join with a slip stitch to top of 3-ch at beginning of round.
Round 5 3 ch and tr4tog over next 4 tr (counts as first cluster), *[5 ch, 1 dc in next 3-ch sp] twice, 5 ch,** 1 cluster over next 5 tr; rep from * 4 more times and from * to ** again, join with a slip stitch top of first cluster.
Round 6 3 ch, 4 tr in first 5-ch sp, [2 ch, 1 dc in next 5-ch sp, 2 ch, 5 tr in next 5-ch sp, 2 ch, 5 tr in next 5-ch sp] 5 times, 2 ch, 1 dc in next 5-ch sp, 2 ch, 5 tr in next 5-ch sp, 2 ch, join with a slip stitch to top of 3-ch at beginning of round.
Fasten off.

To finish all motifs

Weave in any loose ends.
Lay work out flat and gently steam on wrong side.

Stitch diagram
Wagon Wheel

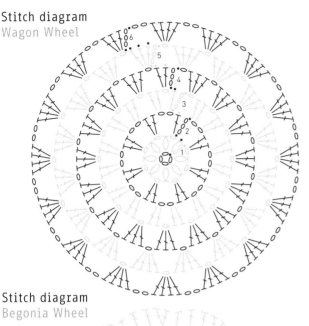

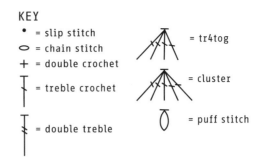

Stitch diagram
Begonia Wheel

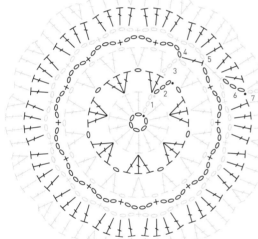

Stitch diagram
Ice Crystal

Masterclass

Tips for working motifs

If you have never attempted making a motif, read the explanation on pages 38–39 about working in rounds. The Wagon Wheel motif is the easiest of the tablemats, so start with this one. It is also a very versatile motif, because you can stop after three rounds for a coaster or work all six rounds for the tablemat.

If you find it difficult to fit all the stitches of the first round into the base ring of the motif, which can happen with thick yarn, undo your work and start again. This time make the chains of the ring loosely or add one or two chains to make it bigger, and leave a long loose end at the beginning. Lay the yarn tail at the back of the motif, level with the chain ring, and work all the stitches of the first round over it – so it is captured inside the base of the stitches. Later you can pull the end to close up the hole at the centre of the ring if you want to. It also means there is less weaving in later.

At the beginning of each round place a stitch marker on the first stitch, a safety pin or a coloured thread will do. If you lose track of which round you are on, simply count the markers. Follow the symbol diagram as you work the rows; it is sometimes easier to understand than the written instructions.

Daisy-chain necklace

This impossibly pretty necklace is created from a long length of chain worked in fine linen yarn, which is embellished with individual leaf and flower motifs. I have added natural shell buttons at irregular intervals to introduce a contrasting texture but in a natural, tonal hue.

Skill level

EASY

In this project you will learn
Practising even chain stitches
Making small flower and leaf motifs
Adding buttons and beads

Stitches used
Chain stitches; Double crochet; Half treble crochet; Treble crochet; Double treble crochet

Size
Approximately 315cm long – but this is easily adjustable to suit desired length

Materials
Anchor Artiste Linen Crochet Thread No. 10,
   a no. 10 linen crochet thread, in one colour:
      1 x 50g ball in natural (shade 392)
2mm crochet hook
16 round two-hole natural shell buttons (eleven
   8mm–11mm; five 14–18mm)

Tension
There is no need to work to a specific tension for this project.

Abbreviations
See page 45.

Special pattern notes
When working the flowers and leaves, leave a long end to use for attaching the motif to the chain. The number of motifs and buttons specified are just a suggestion; alter the numbers as desired.

To make necklace
Using a 2mm hook, work a chain that measures approximately 315cm. Fasten off.
The chain should be long enough to wrap several times around your neck without the need for a clasp.

Five-petal flower (make 13)
Base ring Using a 2mm hook, make 4 chain and join with a slip stitch to first chain to form a ring.
Round 1 1 ch, *1 dc in ring, 3 ch, [yrh and insert hook in ring, yrh and draw a loop through, yrh and draw through first 2 loops on hook] twice, yrh and draw through all 3 loops on hook (called tr2tog), 3 ch; rep from * 4 times more, join with a slip stitch to top of first dc. *5 petals made.*
Fasten off.

Shell-cluster flower (make 2)
Base ring Using a 2mm hook, make 4 chain and join with a slip stitch to first chain to form a ring.
Round 1 *3 ch, 2 tr in ring, 3 ch, 1 slip stitch in last tr worked (one picot made), 1 tr in ring, 3 ch, 1 slip stitch in ring, 3 ch, 3 tr in ring, 3 ch, 1 slip stitch in ring; rep from * once more. *4 petals made.*
Fasten off.

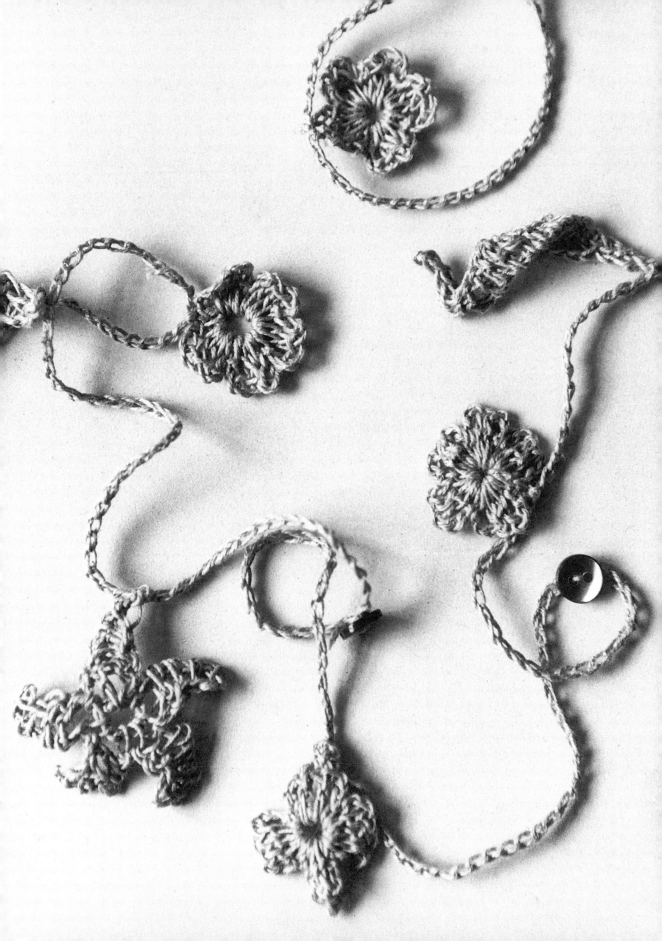

Stitch diagram Small Leaf

Row 1

Pointed flower (make 2)

Base ring Using a 2mm hook, make 4 chain and join with a slip stitch to first chain to form a ring.

Round 1 1 ch, 1 dc in ring, *5 ch, 1 dc in 2nd ch from hook, 1 htr in next ch, 1 tr in each of next 2 ch, 1 dc in ring; rep from * 3 times more, 5 ch, 1 dc in 2nd ch from hook, 1 htr in next ch, 1 tr in each of next 2 ch, join with a slip stitch to top of first dc.
Fasten off.

Small leaf (make 6)

Foundation chain Using a 2mm hook, make 13 chain.

Row 1 Work 1 slip stitch in 2nd ch from hook, 1 dc in next ch, 1 htr in next ch, 1 tr in each of next 2 ch, 1 dtr in each of next 3 ch, 1 tr in next ch, 1 htr into next ch, 1 dc in next ch, 1 slip stitch in last ch.
Fasten off.

To finish

Sew the two ends of the chain together. Weave in any loose ends, leaving the long finishing ends on the motifs.
Using the long ends, sew the motifs randomly to the length of chain. Using a matching sewing threads, sew the small natural shell buttons to the chain, intermingling them between the crochet motifs.

Stitch diagram
Five-petal Flower

Stitch diagram
Shell-cluster Flower

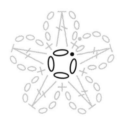

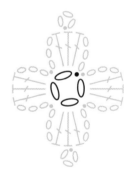

Stitch diagram Pointed Flower

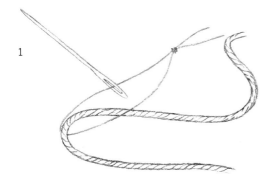

1

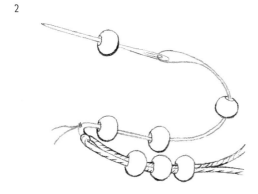

2

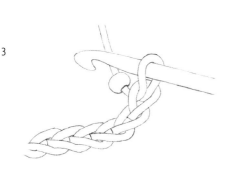

3

4

Crocheting beads and buttons into a chain
If you are crocheting your beads or buttons into the work, rather than sewing them on afterwards, then it is essential that the beads or buttons are threaded onto the yarn before you begin to crochet.

1 Thread a fine sewing needle with sewing thread and make a small knot to join the ends and form a loop. Move the knot so that it is not in line horizontally with the sewing needle.

2 Place the end of the yarn through the loop created by the sewing thread, then pass the beads over the eye of the needle and push down onto the sewing thread and then onto the yarn. The first few beads may be a bit tricky, but so long as the bead holes are large enough, threading will become easier.

3 Make chains up to the point where a bead or button is needed. Then slide the bead or button along the yarn so it sits next to the hook.

4 Work the next chain by wrapping the yarn around the hook beyond the bead or button and drawing it through the loop on the hook.

Patchwork motif blanket

This sumptuous patchwork blanket is entirely made up of the same square motif – 210 motifs, in fact – randomly placed and lovingly oversewn together. Working the separate rounds in one, two, three or four different colours has an intriguing optical effect, breaking up the motif to a greater or lesser degree and accentuating either its rounder or squarer characteristics.

Skill level

INTERMEDIATE

In this project you will learn
Arranging coloured motifs for a patchwork
  effect, see masterclass on page 126

Stitches used
Treble crochet
Double crochet

Size
Approximately 128cm wide x 137cm long

Materials
Rowan Cashsoft 4-Ply, a super-fine-weight
  cashmere-and-wool-mix yarn, in 7 colours:
  A 4 x 50g balls in mauve (446 Quartz)
  B 4 x 50g balls in light brown (456 Arran)
  C 3 x 50g balls in grey (437 Thunder)
  D 5 x 50g balls in pale putty (451 Elite)
  E 5 x 50g balls in turquoise (459 Toxic)
  F 3 x 50g balls in dark brown (432 Bark)
  G 2 x 50g balls in black (422 Black)
2.5mm and 3mm crochet hooks

Tension
Each square measures approximately 9cm x 9cm
using a 3mm hook.

Abbreviations
See page 45.

To make each square motif
See the blanket instructions for the colours.
Base ring Using a 3mm hook and colour required for round 1, make 8 ch and join with a slip stitch to first chain to form a ring.
Round 1 (RS) 3 ch (counts as first tr), 15 tr in ring, join with a slip stitch to top of 3-ch at beginning of round.
Round 2 5 ch (counts as first tr and 2-ch sp), [1 tr in next tr, 2 ch] 15 times, join with a slip stitch to 3rd of 5-ch at beginning of round. *16 spokes.*
Round 3 3 ch (counts as first tr), 2 tr in first 2-ch sp, 1 ch, [3 tr in next 2-ch sp, 1 ch] 15 times, join with a slip stitch to top of 3-ch.
Round 4 1 slip stitch st in each of next 2 tr and next 1-ch sp, 1 ch, 1 dc in same 1-ch sp as slip stitch, *[3 ch, 1 dc in next 1-ch sp] 3 times, 6 ch, 1 dc in next 1-ch sp; rep from * 3 times more, omitting 1 dc at end of last repeat, join with a slip stitch to first dc.
Round 5 3 ch (counts as first tr), 2 tr in first 3-ch sp, [3 tr in next 3-ch sp] twice, *[5 tr, 2 ch, 5 tr] in next 6-ch sp, [3 tr in next 3-ch sp] 3 times; rep from * twice more, [5 tr, 2 ch, 5 tr] in next 6-ch sp, join with a slip stitch to top of 3-ch. Fasten off.

To make patchwork blanket
Make 15 square motifs in each the following 14 colourways, for a total of 210 motifs:
Motif 1 Work each of these motifs in a single colour – 2 in mauve (A), 3 in light brown (B), 3 in grey (C), 2 in pale putty (D), 3 in turquoise (E) and 2 in dark brown (F).
Motif 2 Work these motifs in three colours – round 1 in turquoise (E), rounds 2–4 in pale putty (D), round 5 in dark brown (F).
Motif 3 Work these motifs in two colours – rounds 1–3 in pale putty (D), rounds 4 and 5 in mauve (A).
Motif 4 Work these motifs in three colours – rounds 1 and 2 in black (G), rounds 3 and 4 in pale putty (D), round 5 in turquoise (E).

Motif 5 Work these motifs in three colours – round 1 in pale putty (D), round 2 in black (G), rounds 3–5 in mauve (A).

Motif 6 Work these motifs in two colours – rounds 1–4 in dark brown (F), round 5 in light brown (B).

Motif 7 Work these motifs in three colours – rounds 1 and 2 in mauve (A), round 3 in light brown (B), rounds 4 and 5 in dark brown (F).

Motif 8 Work these motifs in three colours – round 1 in dark brown (F), rounds 2 and 3 in turquoise (E), rounds 4 and 5 in pale putty (D).

Motif 9 Work these motifs in two colours – rounds 1 and 2 in turquoise (E), rounds 3–5 in light brown (B).

Motif 10 Work these motifs in three colours – rounds 1 and 2 in pale putty (D), rounds 3 and 4 in mauve (A), round 5 in grey (C).

Motif 11 Work these motifs in three colours – rounds 1 and 2 in grey (C), rounds 3 and 4 in black (G), round 5 in turquoise (E).

Motif 12 Work these motifs in four colours – round 1 in black (G), round 2 in grey (C), rounds 3 and 4 in turquoise (E), round 5 in light brown (B).

Motif 13 Work these motifs in three colours – round 1 in turquoise (E), rounds 2–4 in grey (C), round 5 in pale putty (D).

Motif 14 Work these motifs in two colours – rounds 1–4 in turquoise (E), round 5 in grey (C).

To finish

Weave in any loose ends.

Lay motifs out flat and gently steam on wrong side. Arrange the motifs into 15 rows of 14 squares (see masterclass).

Sew together the 14 squares in each of the 15 rows to form 15 strips, using small, neat overcast stitches and different coloured yarns.

Then join the 15 strips together in the same way.

Edging

Using a 2.5mm hook, work edging as follows:

Round 1 (RS) Using light brown (B), join yarn with a slip stitch to any tr along outside edge of blanket, 1 ch, 1 dc in same tr as slip stitch, then work 1 dc in each tr, 1 dc in each space either side of seams joining the motifs together, and [1 dc, 1 ch, 1 dc] in each blanket corner to end, join with a slip stitch to top of first dc. Fasten off.

Round 2 Using turquoise (E), join yarn with a slip stitch to any dc of previous round, 1 ch, 1 dc in same dc as slip stitch, then work 1 dc in each dc, and [1 dc, 1 ch, 1 dc] in each blanket corner to end, join with a slip stitch to top of first dc. Fasten off.

Round 3 Using black (G), rep round 2. Fasten off.

Masterclass

Arranging coloured motifs for a patchwork effect

To create a patchwork-effect blanket, take your time when arranging the finished motifs. Lay them out on a flat surface in 15 rows of 14 motifs each. You will find that there are many pleasing arrangements possible; for example, you can arrange all the same motif colourways together to create blocks of colour. In my arrangement, however, I was aiming for a soft, random effect. I used one square of each of the 14 colourways in each of the 15 rows of squares, making sure that the same colourways never touched.

Stitch diagram Square Motif

KEY

•	= slip stitch	+	= double crochet
○	= chain stitch		= treble crochet

Star tablecloth

This decorative centrepiece is made up of repeated star motifs, multiplied to create a hexagonal cloth in which the negative spaces are as important to the overall effect as the positive shapes. The motifs are joined together as you work, leaving minimal finishing.

Skill level

EXPERIENCED

In this project you will learn
Joining shaped motifs as they are worked

Stitches used
Double crochet
Half treble crochet
Treble crochet

Size
Approximately 70cm in diameter

Materials
Anchor Artiste Linen Crochet Thread No. 10,
  a no. 10 linen crochet thread, in one colour:
     3 x 50g balls in natural (shade 392)
2.5mm crochet hook

Tension
Each motif measures approximately 7cm in diameter.

Abbreviation
See page 45.

To make tablecloth
The tablecloth is started at the centre with a single star motif, then as the motifs are made they are joined onto the previous motifs. The diagrams show how the stars are added on – outwards around the centre in rounds.

Centre star motif
Base ring Using a 2.5mm hook, make 9 ch and join with a slip stitch to first chain to form a ring.
Round 1 (RS) 1 ch, 18 dc in ring, join with a slip stitch to top of first dc.
Note: Do not turn at end of rounds but continue with RS of motif always facing.
Round 2 *9 ch, 1 dc in 4th ch from hook, 1 htr in each of next 2 ch, 1 tr in each of next 3 ch, miss next 2 dc on ring, 1 slip stitch in next dc; rep from * 5 times more, working last slip stitch in same dc as slip stitch on previous round.
Fasten off.

Stitch diagram Star

KEY
- •   = slip stitch
- o   = chain stitch
- +   = double crochet
- T   = half treble crochet
- Ŧ   = treble crochet

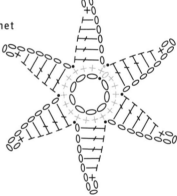

First round of motifs
Join the next six motifs to the centre motif in a round around the centre as shown in the diagrams as follows:
Work the first of these six motifs as for the centre motif, but join the first two legs of this motif to the centre motif as it is being worked. To do this, work the 9-ch of the first leg, carefully remove the hook from the loop and insert it through the 3-ch loop at the tip of one leg of the centre motif, then pull the last loop of the 9-ch through the 3-ch loop and continue down the chain as instructed. Repeat this for the next

leg, then finish the motif in the normal way. Joining on motifs anticlockwise around the centre motif, work the second motif joining the first two legs to the centre motif as before but also join the 3rd leg to the last leg worked on the first motif as shown on the diagram.

Repeat until you have attached six motifs all around the centre motif, joining the last leg of the sixth motif to the third leg of the first motif in this round of motifs.

First motif of first round

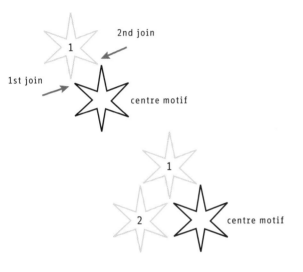

Star tablecloth Motif Placement

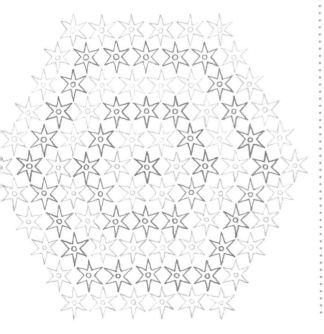

Remaining rounds of motifs

Continue making and joining on motifs in rounds around the centre – join on 12 motifs in the second round, 18 in the third, 24 in the fourth, 30 in the fifth and 36 in the sixth (the last round is not shown on the diagram below).

Note: Make sure you join the legs on the motifs to the legs of the adjacent motifs where they touch as shown in the diagram.

To finish

Weave in any loose ends.

Masterclass

Crocheting motifs together

As well as avoiding having to sew countless motifs together, joining each motif at the connecting points means that you can build the overall shape of the textile as you work.

Make the centre motif. Begin the first motif of the first round but join the first two legs to the centre motif as it is being worked. To do this, work the 9 chain of the first leg, carefully remove the hook from the loop and insert it through the 3-chain loop at the tip of one leg of the centre motif, then pull the last loop of the 9 chain through the 3-chain loop and continue down the chain as instructed. Repeat this for the next leg, then finish the motif in the normal way.

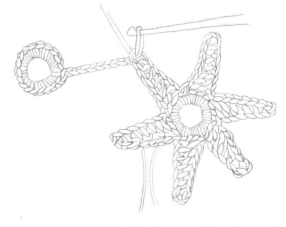

Asymmetrical cardigan

Nobody quite knows the origins of crochet but one of its earliest forms was as simulated lace, hence it was known as crochet lace or chain lace. For this throw-on cardigan, I have put a selection of crochet motifs under the microscope, enlarging them to create this overscaled lace design.

Skill level

EXPERIENCED

In this project you will learn
Joining random-shaped motifs
Working with super-chunky wool yarn

Stitches used
Double crochet; Half treble crochet;
Treble crochet; Treble crochet bobbles;
Treble crochet clusters

Size
One size
Finished measurements
Around bust 122cm
Around sleeve 48cm
Length from shoulder 60cm
From sleeve edge to sleeve edge 112cm

Materials
erika knight Maxi Wool, a super-chunky-weight
    wool yarn, in one colour:
        9 x 100g hanks in ecru (Flax 002)
10mm crochet hook
Large sheet of dressmaker's pattern paper

Tensions
Daisy bloom motif 18.5cm in diameter using a
10mm hook.
Canterbury bell motif 12cm in diameter using a
10mm hook.
Wheel motif 14.5cm in diameter using a 10mm
hook.
Small flower motif 11cm in diameter using a
10mm hook.

Abbreviations
1 bobble = [yrh and insert hook in dc, yrh and
draw a loop through, yrh and draw through first
2 loops on hook] 5 times all in same dc, yrh and
draw a loop through all 6 loops on hook.
tr2tog = [yrh and insert hook in next tr, yrh
and draw a loop through, yrh and draw through
first 2 loops on hook] twice, yrh and draw a loop
through all 3 loops on hook.
1 cluster = [yrh and insert hook in 1-ch sp, yrh
and draw a loop through, yrh and draw through
first 2 loops on hook] 3 times all in same 1-ch sp,
yrh and draw a loop through all 4 loops on hook.
See also page 45.

Special note
The cardigan is made up of 59 motifs. The motifs
are worked individually and then sewn together
into the cardigan shape.

To make daisy bloom motif (make 16)

Base ring Using a 10mm hook, make 8 ch and join with a slip stitch to first chain to form a ring.
Round 1 (RS) 3 ch (counts as first tr), 1 tr in ring, [6 ch, 3 tr in ring] 4 times, 6 ch, 1 tr in ring, join with a slip stitch to top of 3-ch at beginning of round.
Note: Do not turn at end of rounds but continue with RS of motif always facing.
Round 2 *1 ch, work [1 dc, 1 htr, 7 tr, 1 htr, 1 dc] all in next 6-ch sp, 1 ch, miss 1 tr, 1 slip stitch in next tr (centre tr of 3-tr group); rep from * 4 times more, working last slip stitch in top of 3-ch at beginning of previous round.
Fasten off.

Stitch diagram Daisy Bloom Motif

KEY

- • = slip stitch
- ○ = chain stitch
- + = double crochet
- ⊤ = half treble
- ⊤ = treble crochet

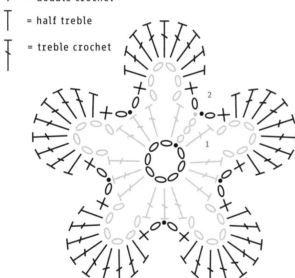

To make Canterbury bell motif (make 12)

Base ring Using a 10mm hook, make 6 ch and join with a slip stitch to first chain to form a ring.
Round 1 (RS) 1 ch, 12 dc in ring, join with a slip stitch to first dc.
Note: Do not turn at end of rounds but continue with RS of motif always facing.
Round 2 3 ch, [yrh and insert hook in same dc as last slip stitch, yrh and draw a loop through, yrh and draw through first 2 loops on hook] 4 times all in same place, yrh and draw a loop through all 5 loops on hook (counts as first bobble), *5 ch, miss 1 dc, 1 bobble (see Abbreviations) in next dc; rep from * 4 times more, 5 ch, join with a slip stitch to top of first bobble. Fasten off.

Stitch diagram Cantebury Bell Motif

KEY

- • = slip stitch
- ○ = chain stitch
- + = double crochet
- ⬮ = bobble

To make small flower motif (make 18)

Base ring Using a 10mm hook, make 6 ch and join with a slip stitch to first chain to form a ring.
Round 1 (RS) 1 ch, 15 dc in ring, join with a slip stitch to first dc.
Note: Do not turn at end of rounds but continue with RS of motif always facing.
Round 2 [3 ch, tr2tog over next 2 dc, 3 ch, 1 slip stitch in next dc] 5 times, working last slip stitch in first dc of previous round.
Fasten off.

Stitch diagram Small Flower Motif

KEY

- • = slip stitch
- ○ = chain stitch
- + = double crochet
- ⋔ = tr2tog

To make wheel motif (make 13)

Base ring Using a 10mm hook, make 4 ch and join with a slip stitch to first chain to form a ring.

Round 1 (RS) 4 ch (counts as first tr and a 1-ch sp), [1 tr, 1 ch] 11 times in ring, 1 slip stitch in 3rd of 4-ch at beginning of round.

Note: Do not turn at end of rounds but continue with RS of motif always facing.

Round 2 1 slip stitch under next ch (the first 1-ch sp), 3 ch, [yrh and insert hook in 1-ch sp, yrh and draw a loop through, yrh and draw through first 2 loops on hook] twice all in same 1-ch sp as last slip st, yrh and draw a loop through all 3 loops on hook (counts as first cluster), [3 ch, 1 cluster (see page 133) in next 1-ch sp] 11 times, 3 ch, join with a slip stitch to top of first cluster.
Fasten off.

Stitch diagram Wheel Motif

KEY

• = slip stitch

o = chain stitch

┬ = treble crochet

⋔ = cluster

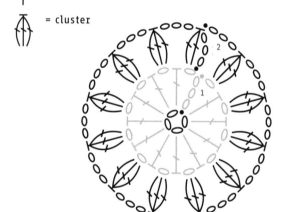

To finish cardigan

Weave in any loose ends.

Lay motifs out flat and gently steam motifs on wrong side.

Following the dimensions on the diagram, draw the cardigan shape on a sheet of dressmaker's pattern paper. Position the motifs right side up on top of the paper pattern shape as indicated on the diagram and as close together as possible – nudge the motifs into shapes that allow them to fit together tightly and touch their neighbours. Pin the motifs in position on the paper.

Sew the motifs together with overcast stitches, leaving all the motifs pinned to the paper until you have finished sewing them together. Remember to leave a opening about 25.5cm long at the centre for the neck opening and from the neck to the bottom edge on the front for the cardigan opening.

Remove the pins and sew the side and sleeve seams with right sides together.

Masterclass

Meshing motifs together

Motifs are deceptively pliable when it comes to meshing them together to make a larger piece, such as this cruxiform shape that makes up the cardigan. Always work on a flat, clean surface such as a table. I don't recommend using the floor as carpets and other floor coverings can create an uneven surface. Before sewing them together, lightly steam each motif to enhance the yarn and highlight the individual shapes. Once all the motifs are laid out, squish them together to achieve the required overall shape. At each connecting point, oversew the motifs together. There will undoubtedly be a few adjustments necessary.

Asymmetrical cardigan
Motif Placement

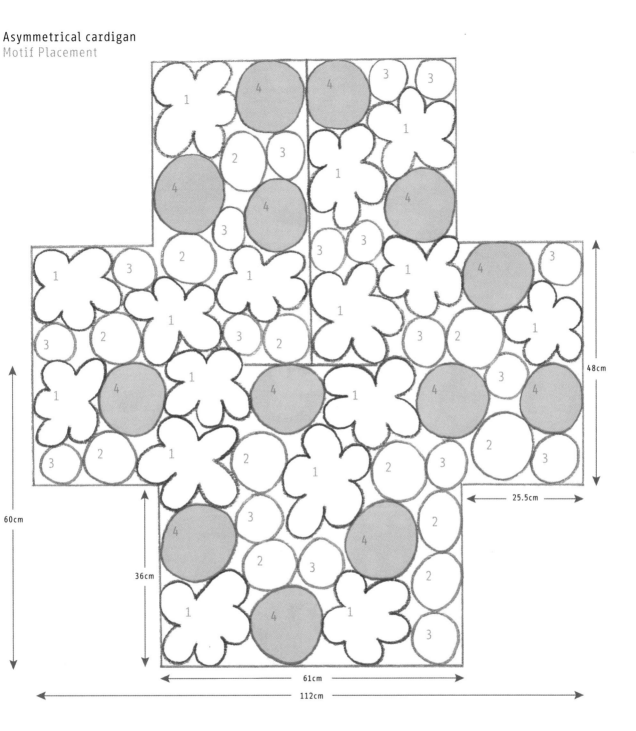

KEY
1 = daisy bloom motif
2 = canterbury bell motif
3 = small flower motif
4 = wheel motif

Edgy stitch scarf

There is a raft of crochet stitches used to add decorative edges to textiles. I have taken a fresh look at traditional edgings, working one of my favourite 'popcorn' stitches in a chunky yarn to create a long length to wear wrapped around the neck as a pretty scarf.

Skill level

EXPERIENCED

In this project you will learn
Working popcorns, see masterclass on page 141
Working a heading along an edging

Stitches used
Double crochet; Treble crochet;
Treble crochet popcorns

Size
Approximately 10.5cm wide x 190cm long

Materials
erika knight Vintage Wool, a chunky-weight wool
    yarn, in one colour:
        4 x 50g hanks in ecru (Flax 002)
5mm and 5.5mm crochet hooks

Tension
Working to an exact tension is not essential for this project.

Abbreviations
1 popcorn at beginning of row = 3 ch, work 6 tr in first sp, remove loop from hook and insert hook from front through top of 3-ch, pick up dropped loop and draw it through, 1 ch to secure popcorn.
1 popcorn = work 7 tr in next sp, remove loop from hook and insert hook from front through top of first of these 7-tr, pick up dropped loop and draw it through, 1 ch to secure popcorn.
See also page 45.

To make scarf
The edging is worked in a strip of half-circle motifs, then the heading is added along one edge.
Edging
Base ring Using a 5.5mm hook, make 10 ch and join with a slip stitch to first chain to form a ring.
Row 1 (RS) 3 ch (counts as first tr), 14 tr in ring, turn.
Row 2 5 ch (counts as 1 tr, 2 ch), miss first 2 tr, 1 tr in next tr, [2 ch, miss 1 tr, 1 tr in next tr] 6 times, working last tr of last repeat in 3rd of 3-ch at end of row, turn.
Work popcorns across next row, making the first popcorn as explained in Abbreviations and the remaining 6 popcorns with 7-tr in normal way.
Row 3 (popcorn row) Work 1 popcorn at beginning of row, [3 ch, 1 popcorn in next 2-ch sp] 6 times, working last popcorn of last repeat in 5-ch sp, turn.
Row 4 10 ch, miss first 2 sps, work [1 dc, 5 ch, 1 dc] all in next 3-ch sp, turn.
Row 5 3 ch (counts as first tr), 14 tr in 5-ch sp, turn.
Repeat rows 2–5 until work measures 190cm from beginning, ending with a row 3 (a popcorn row) – but do not fasten off and do not turn at end of last row.
Heading
Continue along side edge with RS facing and work heading as follows:
Heading row 1 3 ch, 1 dc in 5-ch sp formed at beg of row 2 of pattern, *5 ch, 1 dc in 10-ch sp formed at beg of row 4 of pattern, 5 ch, 1 dc in 5-ch sp formed at beg of row 2 of pattern; rep from * to end, turn.
Heading row 2 1 ch, 1 dc in first dc, *5 dc in next 5-ch sp, 1 dc in next dc; rep from * to end, turn. Change to a 5mm hook.
Heading row 3 1 ch, 1 dc in first st, *3 ch, miss 1 st, 1 dc in next st; rep from * to end.
Fasten off.

To finish
Weave in any loose ends.
Lay scarf out flat and steam very gently on wrong side.

Masterclass

The stitch pattern used for this scarf includes popcorn stitches.

Working popcorn stitch
Popcorn stitches add raised texture to otherwise flat surfaces.

1 When you come to the first popcorn row on the scarf (row 3), begin by working 3 chain.

2 Work 6 trebles into the first 2-chain space of the previous row.

3 Carefully drop the loop from the hook and insert the hook from the front to the back through the top of the 3-chain at the beginning of the row.

4 Then pick up the dropped loop.

5 Draw the loop through the chain.

6 Work 1 chain to secure the 'popcorn'.

7 Work 3 chain, then work 7 trebles into the next space. Drop the loop from the hook.

8 Insert the hook from the front through the top of the first of these 7 trebles, pick up the dropped loop then complete and secure the 'popcorn' as before. Work the following 7-treble popcorns of the row in the same way.

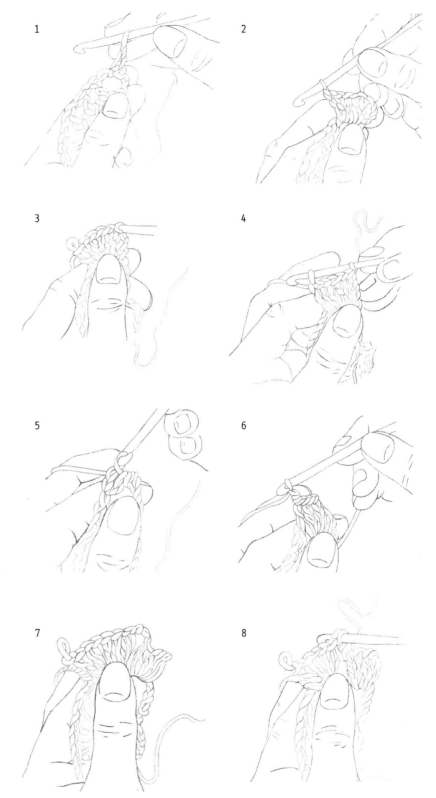

1

2

3

4

5

6

7

8

Recommended yarns

There is a yarn specified for each of the designs in the Project Workshops section of this book. If you are sticking to the recommended yarn, just pick your preferred shade. However, if you are using a different yarn to that specified you must compare the tensions given to ensure the finished result will not wildly differ.

There are standard weights – or thicknesses – of yarns, recognised throughout the spinner's industry. Hand-knit yarns commonly range from 4-ply (fingering) through double knitting (sport weight) to super bulky at the opposite end of the scale. Within each of these categories there is a degree of tolerance, so it is still important to check the tension of each yarn against that given in a pattern (see Checking Your Tension, page 41).

Each yarn will have slightly varying physical properties from the next and will perform differently. Some yarns may be colourfast and easycare whilst others may only be suitable for drycleaning or could possibly felt if not treated correctly. The care information for a yarn will be given on the ball band that comes wrapped around a ball, hank or skein. I always keep a ball band for each project that I make – and if I give a hand knit as a gift, I include the ball band so the recipient knows how to care for the item. When you invest so much of your time and energy into creating a hand-made item, great care should be taken in the laundering.

Alongside the manufacturer's brand name and the name given to the specific yarn, a ball band will typically carry the following information:

Recommended tension and needle sizes
This is the recommended tension and needle or hook size, however a designer may vary from this recommendation within a pattern. If so, always go with the designer's recommendation.

Weight of yarn
Given in grams in the UK and ounces in the US, most yarns come in either 50g or 100g balls.

Meterage
This is the approximate length of yarn in the ball and is just as important to consider as tension when considering a substitute yarn.

Fibre composition
A ball band will list the materials that the yarn is made from, whether that is 100% pure wool or a blend of fibres such as cotton and silk. This affects not just the method of care for the finished item, but also the suitability of a yarn for a certain project.

Shade and dye-lot numbers
Each shade of yarn is given an identifying name and/or number by the manufacturer. When purchasing yarn the dye-lot numer is equally, if not more important, as this number needs to be the same on every ball. As yarn is dyed in batches, buying yarn with the same dye-lot numbers ensures there will be no colour variations between balls.

Care instructions
A ball band will indicate whether the yarn is suitable for machine washing or is dry clean only, and whether or not it can be ironed and, if so, at what temperature. This information is usually given in the form of internationally recognised standard care symbols.

Anchor Artiste Linen Crochet Thread No.10
A fine-weight linen yarn; 100% pure linen; 265m/289yd per 50g/1³/₄oz; recommended crochet hook size — 1.5mm to 2mm.

Erika Knight Maxi Wool
A super-chunky-weight wool yarn; 100% pure wool; 80m/87yd per 100g/3¹/₂oz; recommended crochet hook size — 8mm to 12mm. www.erikaknight.co.uk

Erika Knight Vintage Wool
A chunky-weight wool yarn; 100% pure wool; 87m/95yd per 50g/1³/₄oz; recommended crochet hook size — 5mm to 5.5mm. www.erikaknight.co.uk

Ingrid Wagner Big Knit Yarn
A thrum yarn consisting of a continuous 2.5cm-/1in-wide strip of patterned woven wool fabric — an industrial selvedge edge; 100% pure wool; 21m/23yd per 500g/17¹/₂oz; recommended crochet hook size — 25mm. www.ingridwagner.com

Rico Essential Cotton DK
A double-knitting-weight cotton yarn; 100% mercerised cotton; 130m/142yd per 50g/1³/₄oz; recommended crochet hook size — 4mm.

Rowan Baby Alpaca DK
A light double-knitting-weight alpaca yarn or any alternative alpaca or DK weight yarn to the same specification; 100% baby alpaca; 100m/109yd per 50g/1³/₄oz; recommended crochet hook size — 4mm. www.knitrowan.com

Rowan Cashsoft 4-Ply
A super-fine-weight cashmere-merino blend yarn or any alternative 4 ply weight yarn to the same specification ; 10% cashmere, 57% extra-fine merino wool, 33% acrylic microfiber; 160m/175yd per 50g/1³/₄oz; recommended crochet hook size — 3mm. www.knitrowan.com

Rowan Cotton Glacé
A fine-weight cotton yarn; 100% cotton; 115m/126yd per 50g/1³/₄oz; recommended crochet hook size — 3.25mm to 3.75mm. www.knitrowan.com

Rowan Fine Lace
A lace-weight alpaca-merino blend yarn; 80% baby suri alpaca, 20% fine merino wool; 400m/437yd per 50g/1³/₄oz; recommended crochet hook size — 2mm to 4mm. www.knitrowan.com

Rowan Handknit Cotton
A double-knitting-weight cotton yarn; 100% cotton; 85m/93yd per 50g/1³/₄oz; recommended crochet hook size — 4mm to 4.5mm.
or
Erika Knight Gossypium Cotton
A double-knitting weight cotton yarn; 100% cotton; 100m/109yds per 50g; recommended crochet hook size – 3.5mm to 4.5mm. www.erikaknight.co.uk

Rowan Creative Linen
A double-knitting-weight linen and cotton blend yarn; 50% linen, 50% cotton; 200m per 100g; recommended crochet hook size – 4mm to 4.5mm. www.knitrowan.com
or
Erika Knight studio linen
A double-knitting-weight blend of recycled and premium linen yarn; 85% viscose (recycled linen), 15% linen; 120m/131yds per 50g; recommended crochet hook size – 3.5mm to 4mm. www.erikaknight.co.uk

Yeoman's Cotton Cannele 4-Ply
A super-fine-weight cotton yarn; 100% mercerized cotton; 875m/957yd per 245g/8³/₄oz; recommended crochet hook size – 2.75mm.

Templates for Slipper Boots
(see pages 92–95)

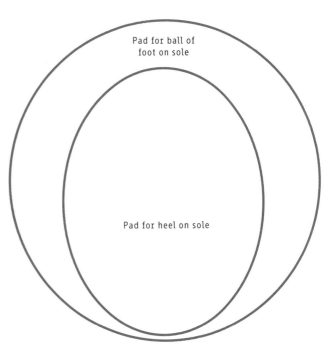

Pad for ball of foot on sole

Pad for heel on sole

Acknowledgements

Once again the simple ethos of the projects in this book belies the complex nature of putting a title like this together. I have been privileged to work with some of the publishing and craft world's best professionals, industry experts of the highest calibre with the most discerning eyes, exacting standards, meticulous attention to detail and above all unbelievable patience, for which I am enormously grateful and I would like to extend my heartfelt appreciation for their huge contributions. This book would certainly not have happened without them.

The truly wonderful team at Quadrille Publishing. To my Publisher and Publishing Director, Alison Cathie and Jane O'Shea. To my Editor Lisa Pendreigh — my sincerest thanks for her professionalism, exceptional patience and personal support — as well as designers Claire Peters and Nicola Davidson for their creative and yet exacting design. And to Aysun Hughes for doing such a fabulous job in the production of the book.

It has been a thrill to work again with photographer Yuki Sugiura; her natural sense of style is central to the sensibility of this book. And, of course, Kim for assisting. My thanks, too, to our stylist Charis for her diligence in the detail. And not forgetting the adorable Panda for so beautifully modelling the pet bed.

To my brilliant project maker, problem solver and personal friend Sally Lee; I am enormously grateful for her misspent — or rather well-spent — youth crafting, knitting, sewing and making stuff, all of which has paid off. And, of course, to Sally Harding, for her inestimable and meticulous work in pattern checking.

As people who know me will testify, I pour over each and every detail endlessly. The choice of yarn is always paramount to me, but most especially when designing and offering projects of simple design. Hence my sincerest thanks and appreciation to the following creators of exceptional yarns of rare distinction for their generosity and enthusiastic support: Rowan, the iconic yarn brand, Anchor, Ingrid Wagner and Yeoman's Yarns for constantly producing desirable fibres and yarns of excellent quality which entice and excite the creative soul. Long may you continue to do so.

Finally this book is dedicated to creatives and crafters everywhere, especially to the new breed of artisan entrepreneurs who are emerging and growing in number and confidence: who continually excite with their passion for the handmade, who constantly push the boundaries of craft with their enthusiasm, innovation and origination.

The future is yours.

Publisher's Acknowledgements
The publisher would like to thank the following for loaning accessories and other items:

LAUREN DENNEY
www.laurendenney.com

ERCOL
www.ercol.com